OPERA IN CRISIS

OPERA IN CRISIS

TRADITION, PRESENT, FUTURE

by
Henry Pleasants

THAMES AND HUDSON

First published in the United States in 1989 by
Thames and Hudson Inc., 500 Fifth Avenue,
New York, New York 10110

Library of Congress Catalog Card Number 89-50541

Typeset in Monophoto Van Dijck
Printed and bound in Great Britain

Contents

Preface

T HESE essays, or articles, are drawn from a variety of books and periodicals, some of them dating back twenty-odd, or even thirty-odd years. Each has been re-read, re-edited, re-typed, revised, expanded, cut and/or updated for this publication.

"Opera in Crisis (1)" is drawn from a chapter, "The Afro-American Epoch," in my book *Serious Music – And All That Jazz!* (1969). "Opera in Crisis (2)" is an updating from a chapter, "The Crisis of Opera," in my *The Agony of Modern Music* (1955), subsequently incorporated in my *Death of a Music? – The Decline of the European Tradition and the Rise of Jazz* (1961) (UK).

"The Plague: Produceritis" is a substantially extended version of an article published under the heading "New Look, New Vandalism?" in the April–May, 1982, issue of the now defunct *Performance* magazine. It has been expanded here to include extracts from my own and others' contributions to the *New York Times*, *Opera* magazine, *Opera News*, the London *Times*, and the London *Daily Telegraph*. "Ordeal by (Tele)Vision" also first appeared in *Performance*.

"Evviva L'Appoggiatura!" is greatly extended from an article in the Christmas, 1986, issue of *About the House*, the magazine of the Friends of Covent Garden. "Of Pitch and Transposition" comes from *About the House* (July, 1981), the article itself drawing on an earlier article, "How High the Gs?" which opened in *Music and Musicians* (December, 1969) and *Opera News* (February, 1971). "Too Early – or Too Late?" also appeared, as "Now and Then," in *About the House* (summer 1983).

"The Lowdown on High Notes" originated in *Stereo Review* (November, 1967), as did "A Vocabulary of Vocalism" (May, 1971). "Opera as Propaganda" first appeared in *Opera News* (February, 1978). "Tracking Down the First and Oldest Recorded Singing Voice" is repeated from *Recorded Sound*, Journal of the British Library Sound Archive, No. 85, January, 1984).

"A Centenary the Met Overlooked" and "The Vienna Decade" are new. "Record or Perish" first appeared as "Giuseppina Cobelli – a Personal Memoir" in *Opera Quarterly*, Vol. 3, No. 4, winter of 1985/86. "The State of the (Vocal) Art" is drawn from the "Coda" of the 1981 reprinting of my *The Great Singers – From the Dawn of Opera to Our Own Time.*

I

Opera in Crisis (1)

T HE crises of opera have been many, reflecting over a span of nearly four centuries a succession of dominant influences: the scenic designer, the singer, the composer, the orchestra, the conductor and, today, the producer. Each has had its triumphs and gone on to overplay its hand and outstay its welcome. But a more fundamental crisis today – and it has been with us ever since Puccini laid down his pen before finishing the last measures of *Turandot* – arises from the question of opera's continuing validity as a living art form.

The crisis has been shared, of course, by every other manifestation of what we think of conventionally as classical or Serious music. In every category we have an inherited repertoire of works from a glorious European tradition, still popular and supported by a vast lay public, but with almost nothing new that has proved capable of establishing itself in the affections of that public.

It is impossible, therefore, and certainly would be ill advised, to consider this fundamental crisis of opera without first placing it in the perspective of the crisis of classical or Serious music as a whole.

The history of Western (essentially European) music conventionally identifies a succession of more or less clearly circumscribed epochs, e.g., Medieval, Renaissance, Baroque, Rococo, Classic, Romantic and Modern, the last of these dating from about 1910 and continuing into the present.

These terms, satisfactory as they may be as symbols of stylistic and conceptual phenomena, give no hint of the succession of national and cultural dominions associated with each major epoch. The Renaissance, for instance, was dominated by the Netherlands, the Baroque by Italy, the Classic by Austria-Bohemia and the Romantic by Germany. It is this phenomenon, historically noted and fully documented, but critically slighted, that may provide, in my opinion, a clue to a better understanding of what has happened and is still happening in our own century.

If we look for a corresponding national dominion – and a continuity of the pattern of successive national or cultural dominions – we can find persuasive evidence that in this century we have been living through – and failing to recognize or declining to acknowledge – what future musical historians may well designate the Afro-American epoch, as represented by a succession of Afro-American musical idioms: ragtime, jazz (in its manifold styles and idioms), blues, rhythm and blues, gospel, rock, the American musical theater and the various and varied hybrids characteristic of the functional music composed for the cinema, radio and television.

The analogies are obvious, the discrepancies inconsequential and easily rationalized, the differences profound but not irreconcilable. In each case, or epoch, we have the music and the musicians of a single nation or culture proving to be so irresistibly attractive to other nations and other cultures as to determine the musical physiognomy of an entire civilization or age.

Paul Henry Lang's *Music in Western Civilization* (1941) includes full-page maps showing (1) the distribution of Flemish (Netherlands) composers throughout Europe between 1470 and 1550; (2) the distribution of Italian composers throughout Europe and the New World between 1675 and 1750, and (3) the distribution of Austro-Bohemian composers throughout Europe and North America between 1700 and 1775, the chronological overlap reflecting the period of transition from the Baroque to the Classic epoch. Lang could have, and should have, added a fourth map, dated a century later, showing a similar dispersal of German composers, performers and teachers throughout the same area, with a heavy concentration in the United States.

A corresponding map drawn today and showing the dispersal of Afro-American music would have fewer American musicians, black and white, in residence abroad, but it would reflect a similar saturation, and an even more pervasive universality. It would also cover a far greater area, the larger part, in fact, of the terrestrial globe. The discrepancy as to residence abroad is purely technical. Where music was once propagated locally by the individual, it is now propagated generally and instantly by the gramophone record, the radio, the motion-picture sound track and television, supported and stimulated by the jet-borne itinerant musician.

Many American jazz, blues, gospel and rock musicians have established residence in foreign lands for longer or shorter periods, including particularly blacks who have found foreign soil more hospitable than their own. But theirs has been an auxiliary influence. The same is true of the scores of foreign musicians who have emigrated to the United States or who have come as visitors for extended periods. The primary influence was, initially, the gramophone record, which, as far back as the late 1920s and early 1930s, made it possible for thousands of Europeans to become jazz enthusiasts who had never heard a first-class jazz musician in person. Only the gramophone record can account for the astonishing circumstance that Europeans, including the British, were well ahead of Americans in assessing correctly the genius of the first great jazz musicians, notably Sidney Bechet, Louis Armstrong and Duke Ellington, and in distinguishing the *idiomatic* difference between jazz and a popular music derived from traditional European models.

It was Constant Lambert, an Englishman, who in *Music Ho!* (1934) could say of Ellington:

"The real interest of Ellington's records lies not so much in their colour, brilliant though it may be, as in the amazingly skillful proportions in which the colour is used. I do not mean skillful only as compared with other jazz composers, but as compared with so-called highbrow composers. I know nothing in Ravel so dextrous in treatment as the varied solos in the middle of the ebullient 'Hot and Bothered', and nothing in Stravinsky more dynamic than the final section. The combination of themes at this moment is one of the most ingenious pieces of writing in modern music."

Ernest Ansermet, conductor of the Orchestre de la Suisse Romande, had reacted immediately and enthusiastically when he heard Bechet in London in 1919, and in the October 15, 1919, issue of *La Revue Romande* he wrote:

"He is content that what he does gives pleasure, but knows nothing more to say about his art than that he 'goes his own way.' That own way is perhaps the mainstream along which the whole world will be swept tomorrow [*c'est peut-être la grande route où le monde s'engouffrera demain*]."

Others, more prominent and influential than Ansermet at that time, were similarly fascinated by the exotic strains emerging from America, and reacted accordingly, if without the acuity of Ansermet's insight and foresight. During the 1920s and early 1930s, Stravinsky, Milhaud, Ravel, Krenek and others documented their fascination in their own compositions. Their failure to understand, or, perhaps, their reluctance to concede, the true significance of this American music may well have reflected an instinctive awareness that more was afoot than merely an exotic popular fad, far more, indeed, than could be accommodated within their own traditional European frame of reference. In any case, they did not pursue the matter.

Here, for the first time, was a music for which the older European intellectual could claim no authorship, with which he had no sense of hereditary identity, and over which he could exercise no control. He could talk about it, but without the assurance of knowing what he was talking about. He could disparage it as a popular aberration, sometimes respectfully, sometimes not – and this was the habitual tactic of the Serious music establishment –, he could dabble with it or ignore it. But deep down, consciously or subconsciously, he sensed not just another passing childish fad, but an intruder from an alien culture. There had been nothing like it in the long history of Western or European music with the possible exception of the transition from Renaissance to Baroque at the end of the 16th and beginning of the 17th centuries, and even that transition, while more radical than any other, had not been alien.

Those stylistic phenomena in which we recognize the distinguishing characteristic of an epoch, or era, represent, almost by definition, a break with tradition, or at least a departure from convention. But such breaks and departures have rarely been so radical as to destroy or frustrate a sense of cultural continuity, or to suggest an entirely new idiom. In music, the boundaries between one musical epoch and another have been, as a rule, neither finely drawn nor acutely felt. Transition has taken place so gradually, so naturally, so inevitably, and often so nearly imperceptibly, that historians and musicologists are far from unanimous in their conclusions as to just when it began and when it ended.

Beethoven, to be sure, may be felt to represent a radical break with the Classic epoch, and to herald dramatically the new Romantic era. Certainly he created a stir in his own time. But few would contend that even his most adventurous music was not rooted in that of his immediate predecessors, or that there was not, in the music of Haydn, Mozart and Cherubini, a foretaste of what was to come.

Transition has always excited controversy, some of it heated, but usually it has been the kind of controversy that derives from the familiar tensions of liberal versus conservative, progressive versus reactionary. Musical language was always changing, but there was no change in the language. The conservative felt his sense of values threatened, but cultural continuity was not interrupted, however much it may have been abused. Beethoven's *Missa Solemnis* and Ninth Symphony, his last piano sonatas and even his last quartets could be played by the same musicians who had played Mozart and Haydn. They were heard and applauded by the same audiences, and they were discussed and reviewed, often perceptively, by the same critics.

Only in the transition from Renaissance to Baroque, in the evolution of tonal, or diatonic, harmony from modal polyphony, had there previously been a break with the past as radical as that which we have experienced in this century. The earlier transition from an *ars antiqua* to an *ars nova*, which had ushered in the Renaissance epoch in the early decades of the 14th century, had certain similar characteristics, *i.e.*, a humanistic reaction to a music grown doctrinaire and artificial, and the introduction of new technical theories and procedures, or the relaxation of traditional constraints. But only the transition from Renaissance to Baroque and the present transition from European to Afro-American – it is still more juxtaposition than transition – have involved such changes of vocabulary, rhetoric and syntax that one must speak of new languages, however much each new language has retained of the old. And only these two transitions have represented so drastic a shift of esthetic base.

It is no insignificant coincidence, certainly, that the serialists, perverse, in my view, as their deductions and intentions may have been, felt that their method or doctrine of musical composition also represented a new language. The coincidence adds importantly, if only circumstantially, to other evidence that the old language had nothing more to yield, that its communicative resources could no longer fuel the kind of familial evolution that had spawned the Classic and Romantic epochs.

As Ernst Krenek put it, explaining the reactionary flavor of neoclassicism as opposed to serialism in his *Selbstdarstellung* (1948):

"The new simplicity [neoclassicism], as revealed by both older and younger composers, is distinct from similar movements in the past in that it is not restricted to the simplification of structure but reaches back to a previous musical language, namely, tonality. The post-Bach primitives cannot be cited as parallels since the musical language was not changed. It was tonal both before and after. A hypothetical parallel would have the composers of the 17th century, confused by Monteverdi's innovations, going back to the modal style of Palestrina."

The serialists were correct, I believe, in their appreciation of the state of European music at about the turn of the century as representing a rhetorical dead-end, and they were also correct in relating it to a comparable situation at the close of the 16th century. In their own view, they did what had to be done – and, indeed, the only thing that could still be done – to safeguard the continuity of the European tradition. One could, as a serialist, go on writing sonatas, suites, symphonies, concertos, chamber music and opera. The same musicians who played and sang Beethoven and Wagner and Strauss could, with a bit of tortuous reorientation and a lot of hard work, play and sing Schoenberg, Berg, Webern and even Boulez, Stockhausen and Birtwhistle. The language was strange, its syntax contrived and awkward, but it could be taught to those who had grown up in the old tongue. The hallowed institutions and the belief in a living art still progressing could be preserved and sustained.

Their error – and it was a howler of prodigious consequence – was the assumption that the composer, confronted with an evolutionary impasse, could, with the grudging acquiescence of a captive and hopeful audience and a despairing press, call the turn. While they busied themselves with rhetorical theory, the living new language was taking form all about them – but in an alien milieu. What they could not have been expected to anticipate was the decisive participation, for the first time in the history of Western music, of, respectively, a new continent and a new civilization: Africa and America. All previous transitions had taken place within the family, so to speak, and the frictions were comparable to those of contending generations. As Friedrich Blume, in his *Renaissance and Baroque Music* (1967), put it:

"The unity of every period in the history of style is relative. Each takes over an extensive heritage in stylistic forms, means of expression, species of composition, objectives and techniques that it finds readily to hand. One part of this heritage it faithfully perserves and cultivates as an antiquity worthy of respect. Another it little by little lets fall into disuse. Still others it remodels to serve its own intent. In corresponding fashion a dying epoch hands onto the next what it has created, leaving the altered spirit of the new time to make of it what it will."

Nothing of this pattern of continuity was felt in the new indigenous music of America as it began to work its way to the surface of popular consciousness in the late 1920s and early 1930s. It was there, all right, for those who chose to look for it – the scales, the harmony, the song and variation forms and the instruments (although the saxophones were newly prominent, if not new, and the double bass was differently employed, as were the drums and other percussion instruments). Most importantly, it was tonal. But what was new was also too garish, too shocking, too bumptious and, for the ear attuned to traditional European music, too exotic. Indeed, there were many who felt it to be atavistic, even in the diluted form in which it was first heard by most white listeners. Hence the reluctance and the inability of those identified with the European musical tradition to discern or acknowledge any kinship. Appearing as it did without credentials of either precedent or pedigree, its validity and possible ascendancy as an art form were – and for many still are – unthinkable.

This resistance has produced, significantly, a striking parallel with one of the distinctive phenomena of the transition from the Renaissance to Baroque: the coexistence for a considerable period of two incompatible musical idioms. "The old style," says Manfred F. Bukofzer in his *Music in the Baroque Era* (1947), "was not cast aside, but deliberately preserved as a second language, known as the *stile antico* of church music. The hitherto unchallenged unity of style disintegrated, and composers were obliged to become bilingual."

If, today, we were to substitute *stile antico* and *stile moderno* for *serious* and *popular* or for *classical* and *jazz* the pertinence to our own time of Bukofzer's description of coexistence in the 17th century would be obvious, if not in the work of those whose names are associated primarily with new Serious music, then certainly in the music of those who have worked, often brilliantly, as composers for films, radio and television and as arrangers for jazz bands and popular singers, drawing upon both idioms as dictated by setting and substance.

For most of those concerned with music, however, whether professional or amateur, the legitimacy of the comparison is compromised by the conventional view of the Serious composer as a writer of modern music. Those who wrote in the *stile antico* in the 17th century were militant conservatives. But so also, in my view, are today's Serious composers. There conservatism may be masked by a fulsome profession of modernism, but what they write is addressed, however, to an essentially conservative public, hostile to, or ignorant of, any truly modern music.

This public's taste is dominated in the still viable repertoire of the opera house and the concert hall. The composer, in his profession of modernity, the public in its tolerance and sponsorship of new music that it rarely likes, and the critics in their championship of the composer's right to be heard – and financed – and to go on being heard whether his music pleases or not, are allied in what Virgil Thomson, during his tenure as music critic of the New York *Herald Tribune*, described, with engaging candor (14 February, 1954), as "a conspiracy to defend the faith."

Nor is their conservatism solely or even essentially musical. Basically it is institutional, concerned primarily with preserving the symbols of an established social order and with perpetuating an established catalogue of cultural virtues. Most people go to concerts and the opera today just as they go to church, sincere enough in their worship, whether of God or Beethoven, but also savoring the respectability of their attendance and the assumption of connoisseurship.

There are many other parallels between the 17th century and the 20th, and each of them is worth examination. Most obvious, perhaps, is a nearly identical reaction in favour of intimacy and immediacy to a music that had become too complex, too scientific, too overloaded with intellectual contemplation and too remote from the natural lyrical expression of human sentiment and the natural and expressive rhythms of bodily movement. The reaction in the 17th century had been led, to be sure, by intellectuals, and its first composers, as Bukofzer says, tended to be bilingual. The 20-century reaction, as reflected first in ragtime, then in jazz, was led by nobody. But the results have been similar.

What distinguishes the new Afro-American idiom from any previous Western music is nothing but a new concept of rhythm and phrase. But then all that the early Baroque composers did in breaking with the Renaissance was put a new stress to the top and bottom lines of multiple-voiced song and exploit the dramatic implications of the major and minor scales as they emerged from the earlier and less dramatic modes. But it has been felt as sufficiently radical and sufficiently offensive at the time – in each case – to blind the traditionalist to how much of the old was still present in the new, and to excite resistance. If we accept the concept of an Afro-American epoch, then the analogy with a succession of European national and cultural dominions is obvious.

Western music continued to evolve, and still continues to evolve, but the action had moved to a new continent. The cycle of European epochs had run out of steam or, as Hindemith so cogently put it in *A Composer's World* (1953), had run out of new chords. What has been hopefully thought of as further progress has been a carefully nurtured and expensively and tediously propagated delusion. What the BBC, for example, has seen fit to offer year after year as "music in our time" is no such thing. Opera is musical theater, and musical theater survives, but it has been in the American musical and in music written for cinema, radio and television, mercifully ignored by music criticism.

Serious composers, Serious critics and the Serious music community as a whole were mindful of the mistakes attributed to earlier generations in the assessment of new music. Determined not to be caught napping again (the Hanslick syndrome), they welcomed their own new music, often against their better judgment. Like statesmen and military men, they tended to appraise the present in terms of the past, and to make the decisions that should have been made before. And so they concentrated on the wrong novelties and drew the wrong conclusions.

Music critics and music historians – and composers, too – assumed that rejection of, or indifference to, contemporary Serious music by the Serious music audience was simply a matter of history repeating itself, that the new composers, in due course, would be vindicated as Beethoven, Brahms, Wagner and Strauss had all been vindicated. If we date the Modern phase from about 1910, we have a span of eighty years in which vindication has failed to materialize. It is too long a time. Critics, historians and composers had, it seems, committed precisely the error that their sponsorship of the new Serious music was designed to avoid.

History, as usual, fooled the experts. And it fooled them in the usual way. It didn't repeat. Only the experts repeated.

2

Opera in Crisis (2)

T HE music familiar to most of us as western or Classical or Serious dates from the turn of the 17th century. It was born, if not in the opera house, then in a new kind of musical theater that caused opera houses to be built. This musical theater represented a reaction by its founders – Peri, Caccini, Monteverdi *et al.* – against what was felt to be the artificiality and excessive complexity of the preceding polyphonic era. It favoured a music more closely related to, and rooted in, the rhythms and melodic contours and cadences of speech, a lyrical extension and sublimation of the rudimentary music of verbal communication beyond that already achieved in poetry, where, when voiced, the sound is sustained and shaded in a songful fashion.

Coincidental with this new realization of the communicative musical properties of speech came an appreciation of the dramatic implications of the emergent diatonic major and minor scales and the manner in which these implications or properties could be supported and reinforced by a sequence of chords providing stimulating contrasts of consonance and dissonance – in other words, diatonic and subsequently chromatic harmony.

Although the evolution of post-Renaissance European music has been dominated by the trend from an originally vocal art to an ultimately instrumental art, opera has remained one of its principal representative forms. All the evolutionary factors in European music have been present in the evolution of opera, and many of them originated in opera.

It would be impossible, of course, to write a history of post-Renaissance European music with reference to opera alone, but any satisfactory history of opera will embrace all the evolutionary factors essential to a critical understanding of what transpired. An examination of Monteverdi, Alessandro Scarlatti, Handel, Gluck, Mozart, Cimarosa, Beethoven, Cherubini, Rossini, Weber, Donizetti, Bellini, Meyerbeer, Verdi, Gounod, Massenet, Wagner, Mascagni, Puccini, Strauss, Debussy and Berg would provide all that is needed to describe the arc of the rise and fall of the idiom.

The decisive factors throughout the story are harmony and the orchestra. That it is impossible to list the singer among these factors gives the story a flavour of perversity. We are offered, in boldest outline, the spectacle of an instrumental art born of a vocal art which made a singer of the orchestra and collapsed when the original vocal objective was forgotten.

The singer has remained without influence. At each step along the way he has had to yield to the overriding demands of the orchestra. He has had his moments – or decades – to be sure. There were times in both the 18th and 19th centuries when the singer ruled the roost, and composers did his bidding. But the trend of musical evolution was against him. History records these as bad periods. They were terminated by reform movements born of the conviction that there was more to music and musical theater than song or mere singers could provide.

This "more" was always found in harmony and in the orchestra. The implications of harmony seemed more substantial than the blandishments of a tune, however meltingly or forcefully delivered, and the instrument of harmony, since a vocal chorus could only incidentally be employed, was the multiple-voiced orchestra. The four-century history of opera shows the singer in a long battle with the orchestra, a battle punctuated by dramatic fluctuations, but with the outcome never in doubt. The great – and flamboyant – Angelica Catalini, early in the 19th century, is said to have objected to Mozart on the grounds that in his operas the orchestra functioned like a police escort. As a vocalist she had a point. But it was lost.

The nature of the conflict, and its implications, were not understood even by the protagonists. The reform composers, notably Gluck, Wagner and Verdi, never forgot that in favouring the orchestra they were imposing upon it vocal responsibilities. And the singers who acquiesced in the surrender of their primacy, themselves fascinated by the challenge of orchestra participation, failed to realize that they were losing their life's blood of vocal melody.

Nor were the implications of the conflict apparent to the lay listener. They are not understood to this day. The opera-going public still favours *Il barbiere di Siviglia*, *Lucia*, *Norma*, *Il trovatore*, *Aida*, *Tannhäuser*, *Lohengrin*, *La Bohème* and *Madama Butterfly*, all primarily singers' operas. But few are disposed to challenge the historical judgment of *Otello* or *Falstaff* as Verdi's masterpieces, or of *Tristan und Isolde* and *Parsifal* as Wagner's. One simply deplores the unenlightened condition of public taste. The public accepts the disparagement – and continues to pay allegiance to its favourites.

The low estate of contemporary opera composition, while recognized, is not understood as a consequence of evolutionary forces still enthusiastically applauded. History goes no farther than to note that until the mid-1920s the opera repertoire enjoyed more or less annual enrichment from contemporary composition and that thereafter it did not. New operas were written, hundreds of them, but they too rarely found favour with the opera-going public. There has been little disposition, however, to seek in Wagner, Verdi and Richard Strauss the root of the evil.

Hanslick did when, reviewing the first production of *Der Ring des Nibelungen* in Bayreuth in 1876, he wrote: "The music to *Götterdämmerung* characterizes its author anew as a brilliant specialist, rather adjacent to music than of it. It is unthinkable that his method shall be, as he contends, the absolute 'art work of the future'. When an art arrives at a period of utmost luxury, it is already in decline. Wagner's opera style recognizes only superlatives; but a superlative has no future. It is the end, not the beginning. From *Lohengrin* on, Wagner broke a new path, dangerous to life and limb; and this path is for him alone. He who follows will break his neck, and the public will contemplate the disaster with indifference."

Well, if not with indifference, then certainly with despair and dismay. Characteristic of modern opera generally is the assignment of the musical expressive function to the orchestra and the reduction of the singer to the role of recitative-articulating actor. The idiom of the orchestra, in turn, is what is familiar as modern music, a music that loftily despises song. In this respect the iniquities of modern opera are identical with the iniquities of modern music in general, with the single exception that opera is better suited than other forms to deriving some benefit from the descriptive faculties that came to the fore in the orchestra in the decadence of the idiom.

The contemporary idiom of the singer is the parlando recitative inherited from the last great manifestations of Italian opera (*verismo*) and the declamatory style inherited from Wagner. Gone are the arias, duets, trios, quartets, quintets, sextets, septets, grand finales and grand choruses that so delighted the audiences of Mozart, Beethoven, Weber, Rossini, Donizetti, Bellini, Meyerbeer, Verdi, Puccini – and even Wagner.

All successful operas have succeeded because they have given musical pleasure and excitement, because the audience's attention has been held and its spirit moved by beautiful singing of beautiful melodies, stirring drama, a great spectacle or – as in the case of the most successful operas – by the three in combination. No opera has succeeded that did not give singers something to sing. Cesare Siepi put his finger on it when asked what he had against modern composers. "Nothing," he said. "I just wonder what they have against me."

Opera, as I have noted, owes its existence as an art of the theater to the dramatic implications of tonal harmony, which is why, like the symphony and the symphonic poem, it exists only in European music. Harmony is articulate, however, only in song, whether the singing be entrusted to voices or to instruments. In opera, the singing was initially entrusted to singers, since the purpose was the representation of drama, and the technique the articulation of drama by singing actors. But as the orchestra emerged as the ideal instrument of harmonic music, the singer had to adjust himself to a concept of music that recognized the orchestra as the dominant executive agent.

Modern opera results from interpreting this as a trend directed not only against the singer, but also against song. Overlooked is the fact that in *Tristan und Isolde* and *Otello*, while the orchestra may be dominant, even domineering, it sings. Wagner and Verdi sensed instinctively that there can be no music without song. When they inhibited the singing of their singers by grafting the vocal line to prosaic text, they saw to it that the melodic loss was made good in the orchestra. Their successors simply noted the absence – or increasing rarity and subordination – of set vocal pieces and concluded that Wagner and Verdi had come up with something superior to song.

For sixty years now, composers have given us recitative and parlando operas that disdain the agreeable sensuous communication of song, vocal or instrumental, without substituting for it the precise articulation of the spoken word. They have given us operas that, uncommunicative musically, are dependent for communication upon the text. The singer is restricted to declamation in order that the text may be understood. And then he is drowned out by a clamorous orchestra in order that the composer may still claim to have written an opera.

The composer makes a point of integrating music and drama, and achieves neither one nor the other – nor anything else. If one listens to the music the experience is unrewarding since, as the composer will be the first to proclaim, it is unintelligible without reference to the drama. But if one attends to the drama, nothing comes of it but frustration since the text is normally lost in the orchestral din. And it only takes a flute to frustrate enunciation of text.

The villain of the piece is, of course, Wagner. Modern opera is, like all modern music, reactionary, and no other composer is so stigmatized by the reaction as Wagner. The length of his music dramas, his system of *Leitmotive*, the size and richness of his orchestra, the licentiousness of his chromatic harmonies, the ecstasies of his modulations, the philosophical pretensions of his libretti and their appalling German – all are rejected. But these all have to do with manner rather than with method. Wagner's method – the integration of music and drama with music subordinate to text – has survived. The irony is that no composer ever so flagrantly and successfully violated his own proclaimed method. Wagner's music has survived not because of his method, but in spite of it.

The opera-going public goes to the Wagnerian music-dramas to hear the music – in the orchestra and from the singers on the stage. They go to hear "The Ride of the Valkyries", the "Waldweben", "Wotan's Farewell", "The Magic Fire Music", Wolfram's "Abendstern", Elsa's "Dream", Elisabeth's "Dich teure Halle", Sieglinde's "Du bist der Lenz", Siegmund's "Winterstürme", Brünnhilde's "Immolation", Siegfried's "Funeral March" and "Rhine Journey", Tristan and Isolde's "O sink hernieder Nacht der Liebe" and Isolde's "Liebestod" and so on – all musical episodes of lyric, epic and dramatic grandeur.

Hardly anyone understands the words, unless they have been committed to memory. The audience is required to sit a long time between these musical pleasures. It puts up with a good deal of sheer boredom during those barren patches where Wagner really practiced what he preached. As Hanslick put it: "Generally speaking, one can be certain that with the appearance of so much as the point of Wotan's spear, a half-hour of emphatic boredom is in store." And yet, many consider it worth the tedium, and some are even impressionable enough to persuade themselves that they enjoy the ugly, empty wastes of Wagnerian recitative.

The purely musical basis of Wagner's popularity is something more recent composers have never appreciated. They have held to his method and discarded his manner, not recognizing that what was valid and vital in Wagner was precisely his manner, including particularly the excesses and extravagances the composer of today so heartily despises.

Wagner, as composer, was a musician in spite of himself. He achieved success and immortality in the theater just as Mozart, Rossini, Donizetti, Bellini, Meyerbeer and Verdi did – by writing memorable, singable melodies. He was music's greatest unwitting hypocrite. He was determined to bridle, or at least discipline, the singer. But instinctively he realized the telling effect of a well-prepared high B flat, B or C as the climax of a long melodic line. Wagnerian opera is dominated by the tenor and the prima donna to this day just as any other opera is; indeed, even more so since so few singers can now meet the requirements.

Wagner compounded the paradox by adding a new virtuoso – the conductor. In his music, for the first time, orchestra and singer are on equal footing. When the singer does not sing, the orchestra does. They often sing together. For the orchestra's song the conductor is responsible. Since Wagner's time, with the primacy of the orchestra established, the conductor has been to opera – until the producer came along – what the castrato had been to the opera of the 17th and 18th centuries.

It would probably have been impossible to continue much farther in the Wagnerian direction – that is, in the direction pointed by Wagner's musical as opposed to his theoretical instincts. There had to be a limit to loudness and richness and bigness. Wagner did not reach it. But he came close, and Strauss had no difficulty at all in finishing the job with *Salome*, *Elektra* and *Der Rosenkavalier*.

The contemporary composer's error has been not in failing to take up where Wagner and Strauss left off – there was hardly anywhere to take off to – but in failing to understand what Wagner had been. They were influenced by his theories and his method, and ignored the obvious musical reasons for his success.

They neglected to note that the essential musical nature of opera had not been changed, least of all in the opera house, and that in the opera house, as in the concert hall, vocal melody, or an instrumental substitute for it, remained the alpha and omega of music. It is an axiom that Verdi never overlooked, even in theory. It has made him, for the contemporary composer, a more complicated point of departure.

Despite the great successes scored by singers in Wagner's music-dramas, the impact of his personality, the novelty of his idiom and the evangelistic fervor of its propagation blinded even the sophisticated to the essentially melodic source of his popularity. Hanslick, for instance, for all his insight, and although he recognized and acknowledged the great musical episodes, kept attacking the Wagnerian method as if it were the method that really counted.

Verdi's course from *Nabucco* to *Falstaff* was more gradual, and was accomplished without the fanfare of theoretical revelation and the dogma of a reform platform. But he could not entirely escape the trend of the time. He never lost sight of the singer, but he did, toward the end, begin to slight song. Hanslick felt this when he heard *Otello* in Milan in 1887, shortly after the premiere, and commented:

"Song remains the decisive element, but it follows closely the course of thought, feeling and word. Independent, self-sufficient, symmetrically constructed melodies appear less frequently than does the cross between recitative and cantilena which now dominates modern opera. . . . If the right choice of colour for every mood, and the emphatic notation of every turn of speech were the single objective of opera, then we could unhesitatingly declare *Otello* to be an improvement over *Aida* and Verdi's finest work.

"This devotion to the poem does not, however, release the opera composer from other obligations. He must above all else be a musician, and on this basis we expect music not only in accord with the text, but also attractive to us simply as music – individual, original and self-sufficient. . . . We demand of the opera composer beauty and novelty of musical ideas, particularly melodic ideas. And from this point of view *Otello* strikes me as less adequate than *Aida*, *La traviata* or *Un ballo in maschera*."

To the succeeding generation of Italian composers it did not appear, as it did in the case of Wagner, that Verdi had reached a limit. They reckoned that his was a direction offering reasonable prospect of further profitable vistas. This proved to be the case, if in a limited degree. The job of running out the vein, performed for German opera by Strauss, and for French opera by Debussy and Charpentier, was done for the Italians by Leoncavallo, Mascagni, Giordano, Cilea and Puccini. But again the composers committed a critical error, or, to put it more precisely, an error in criticism.

Their mistake was in thinking of the succession of Verdi's operas in general terms of continuous progress, from crude to good to better to best, the last applying to *Otello* and *Falstaff*. In terms of technical mastery and dramatic sophistication this was certainly the case. The professional composer or critic may find *Otello* superior to *Aida*, and *Falstaff* superior to *Otello*, but as pure music *Aida* is superior to both.

The composers turned to *Otello* and *Falstaff* to find out what Verdi was driving at. They found something much akin to the Wagnerian concept of integrated music-drama, free of Wagner's Germanic trappings. What they failed to understand was that even Verdi could be wrong, or at least go too far. Verdi's destination was *Aida*. He had developed a considerable momentum in getting there, and in *Otello* and *Falstaff* he overshot the objective.

It is easy to understand, at this distance, the temptation *Otello* and *Falstaff* represented. They offered more concentrated, more pointed, more modern pleasure and excitement. The pace is faster, the action more direct and, in the case of *Otello*, more violent and shocking. The form is less conventional. The set pieces have almost vanished. There are some in *Otello*, although less numerous and less conspicuous than in *Aida*. There are fewer in *Falstaff*. *Otello* and *Falstaff* represented, when superficially examined, and from the point of view of the time, a liberation from operatic conventions, a step toward real music-drama, a closer approximation than Wagner was able to achieve of a complete amalgamation of the various arts involved in opera.

Such an appreciation was correct enough, but the conclusions drawn from it were as mistaken as those drawn from the similar appreciation of Wagner, and hardly less disastrous, although easier to condone. Verdi was the more honest progressive of the two, or at least the more consistent, and his results were more convincing. Wagner's visions could be ridiculous; Verdi's never were. He had as good a sense of the theatre as Wagner, and a more conscious understanding of the essentially musical nature of opera. Thus it was tempting to believe that both *Otello* and *Falstaff* owed their success and the high esteem in which they were held to what was new in them rather than to what was old.

This may have been true as far as the critics and the initiated public were concerned. But it was not the new that kept them in the repertoire. It was what still survived of the earlier Verdi. Critics may praise as they will the declamatory style of *Otello*, but what keeps it in the repertoire is the choruses of the first and third acts; Otello's "Esultate" and "Dio, mi potevi scagliar"; the duet with Desdemona at the close of Act I; Iago's Drinking Song and Credo; the Otello-Iago duet at the close of Act II, and Desdemona's Willow Song and "Ave Maria" and Otello's valedictory in Act IV. There are fewer such melodic excursions in *Falstaff*, which is why *Falstaff* is less often in the repertoire than *Otello*.

Contemporary composers would have done better had they not dismissed the fact that *Aida* is still more popular than either *Otello* or *Falstaff* and always will be – assuming that there are singers capable of doing it justice, which must today be a rash assumption. They erred in listening to the critics rather than the box-office. About this, even Verdi, for whom the box-office was never an institution to be taken lightly, may have been deceived. By the time *Otello* was produced he had achieved a position in the hearts of his countrymen and others where failure would have been next to impossible. Verdi, along with the main stream of Serious music, had moved away from his popular base. He, too, had been seduced by the lure of a music that would be more than song.

Here is the tragedy of European music in miniature. In aspiring to more than song its composers denied those very lyric faculties of music which prompt people to express themselves musically, and which make the musical expression of others intelligible. Preoccupied with harmony and instrumentation, they forgot that the musician's primary purpose and usefulness in life is to sing.

The normal means of vocal communication is speech. All speech is coloured by variations of pitch and rhythm employed spontaneously to supplement the precision or imprecision of words with a sense of the feelings associated with them. All speech is in some degree musical, and all speakers composers, in however rudimentary a way. Vocal and verbal communication is never entirely dissociated from musical communication. Musical expression begins when a baby first uses its vocal cords.

Poetry is a lyrical extension of speech. It is distinguished from speech by a rhythmical organization whose purpose is to encourage, support and animate a vocal utterance more consciously and more consistently sustained than is customary or practical in everyday speech.

The advantage of the sustained tone of poetry over the more negligently sustained tone of speech is its plasticity. The melodic variation can be enriched and accentuated. The opportunities for expressive coloration are infinitely increased, if only because the tone is of longer duration and gives the speaker more time for its lyrical exploitation and elaboration. Poetry is, in short, a step toward song. Although an understanding of the words is still essential to a satisfactory communication, the melodic component is on at least a level with the verbal.

If one wishes to go beyond the poet's capacities for sensuous or melodic communication, the next step is song. Here the voice is fully sustained, and the melodic component of the communication dominant, if not exclusive. The words rather cease to count. The communication is sensuous rather than ideational, general rather than precise. The words are hardly more than a guide to the singer. They are helpful but not essential to the listener, which is why songs in all languages are effective everywhere regardless of the language in which they are sung, provided only that they are good songs and well sung.

Song has the advantage over poetry of an immeasurably, incomparably greater range of expressive coloration and emphasis, since the tone can be varied in pitch, augmented or diminished in volume and accelerated or retarded in movement in a purely musical way. Because of sustained plastic, malleable tone, music can work in expressive spheres where prose, bound to the word, and poetry, released from absolute verbal precision but still constrained by text, cannot go, which is why the musician sings – or should.

The course of our European or Serious music since Beethoven's time has been in the opposite direction. Musicians have acted as though music's ideational imprecision were a fault, and as though its salvation lay in finding in it the narrative and descriptive faculties that are the natural attributes of speech, poetry, painting and sculpture. In opera this general tendency has found expression in a denial of purely musical values in favour of textual or descriptive values. Instead of making opera the extension of the theater in song, composers since Wagner's and Verdi's time have tended to make it a theatrical extension of music. They have behaved as if song were something to be ashamed of, and have produced a songless music of which they should be ashamed.

Parlando recitative or dry declamation has replaced the sustained aria and concerted number. Choral commentary has replaced the exuberant song of massed voices. Ballet has been shunned, and as a result opera has been deprived not only of song, but of dance. Even the orchestra, opera's last great singer, has become a humble provider of commas, periods, exclamation points, descriptive colour, inflated dynamic contrasts and mood painting. The faculties of free, emotional, sensuous expression in song, which are music's purest and most treasurable property, have been denied, as if composers were all ascetics and song a cardinal sin.

It is in the opera house that the ascetic character of most 20th-century Serious music is most keenly felt. A symphony or concerto or suite without song may deceive by its thematic workmanship and the skill and ingenuity of its instrumentation. In the opera house, with attention diverted from the orchestra to the stage, the absence of song becomes insupportable, for there is less music in the declamatory idiom of modern opera than in the spoken words of the modern theater.

The kind of declamation or parlando recitative now fashionable defeats rather than assists the musical objective. By restricting the voice to arbitrary pitches in a manner incompatible with the melodic-structural character of song, the composer puts the singer in an emotional straitjacket. The vocal line

27

to which he is constrained offers less opportunity for melodic expression than the flattest sort of speech.

Little has been written in opera in the past fifty or sixty years that could compare as music with any Shakespearean speech, even as delivered by an indifferent actor. An idiom that originated as the creative extension of the rudimentary music of speech has ended in the more radical of its present forms by being less musical than the gurgle of a newborn babe.

3

The Plague: Produceritis

T HE heading: "Singers Upstaged by Set." Beneath it, in a dispatch to *The Times* (London) from Patrick J. Smith in New York, we were told: "At the curtain calls for the new production of *La Bohème* at the Met, James Levine pushed Franco Zeffirelli on stage, then darted off, leaving Zeffirelli to take the solo. The benefit audience gave him the standing ovation usually reserved for star singers."

The mind's eye easily envisages Zeffirelli out there taking his solo curtain call while the mind itself registers this tableau as a vivid reflection of the present state of opera. What had begun as a singer's art nearly four centuries ago was taken over by the conductor, beginning with Hans Richter, Gustav Mahler and Arturo Toscanini, and has now passed to the producer – or director, or director/designer.

For the first half of this century, the conductor was dominant. One spoke of Knappertsbusch's *Ring*, Krauss's *Salome*, Walter's *Le nozze di Figaro*, Busch's *Così fan tutte*, Furtwaengler's *Tristan und Isolde*, Ansermet's *Pelléas et Mélisande*, Kleiber's *Elektra*, and so on. Since the end of World War II it has been Wieland Wagner's *Ring* or *Parsifal* (not Knappertsbusch's), Jean-Pierre Ponnelle's *Falstaff*, Zeffirelli's *Carmen* (not Carlos Kleiber's), Terry Hands's *Parsifal* (even with Solti conducting), Götz Friedrich's *Ring* and *Der Freischütz* (not Colin Davis's), Joachim Herz's *Fidelio*, Peter Hall's *Don Giovanni*, Giorgio Strehler's *Lohengrin* (not Abbado's), etc.

What we have had in the past forty years, beginning with Wieland Wagner in Bayreuth and Walter Felsenstein in East Berlin, has been the operatic Age of the Producer. It has been a bad one, and it has grown worse as producer/ directors have striven to outdo one another in collecting the boos and critical brickbats (not unmixed with distressing critical huzzahs) that make headlines, ensure notoriety and garner further engagements. It has sometimes occurred to me that we may have reached a point in operatic history where a claque is paid to boo.

Some of these producer/directors have even seen fit to turn the opera house into a forum for Marxist propaganda, as Friedrich, Herz and Harry Kupfer, all disciples of Felsenstein, have done with the *Ring*, *Der Freischütz* and *Fidelio* at the Royal Opera, Covent Garden, the English National Opera, the Welsh National Opera and elsewhere. One has wondered why the powers-that-be in these houses have tolerated and even encouraged these lectures on liberation and freedom by producers seemingly untroubled by a wall that denies freedom of movement and utterance to the population of the German Democratic Republic. That wall, after all, was erected not to keep the intruder out, but to keep the inhabitants in. Thus it was with a sigh of surprised relief and a gasp of "At last!" that one read, a few seasons ago in *The Daily Telegraph* under the heading, "Marx Brothers at the Opera": "It is past time that our opera companies ended their love duet with East German producers."

The reference was, of course, to Friedrich, Herz and Kupfer, and was prompted by a Kupfer production of *Fidelio* for the Welsh National Opera in which, according to the *Daily Telegraph's* Alan Blyth: "Poor Anne Evans as Lenore is forced to walk about in a trench coat. . . . Marzelline is an expressionist neurotic, Jaquino . . . is a sadist, surely soon to slip into Pizarro's shoes," etc. The editorial concluded: "Except in the case of works intended as such (those produced by Brecht and Weill, for instance) polemics and the stage make bad bedfellows."

It is not simply a question of polemics, nor are all the miscreants from the German Democratic Republic. Polemics are only an offensive gloss on matters of far greater significance and consequence, as explored a few years ago in a book, *Misdirection: Opera Production in the Twentieth Century* by Alois M. Nagler, the Henry McCormick Professor Emeritus of Dramatic History at Yale University, first published in German as *Malaise in der Oper*.

Professor Nagler's catalogue of horrors includes such delectable items as Jean-Pierre Ponnelle's notion that the central figure of *Der fliegende Holländer* is the helmsman who dreams it all up, and a 1978 production of the same opera in Wuppertal, which updated it to *c*. 1840, turned the sailing vessel into a steamship and had the spinning wheels operated by a machine (not unlike Brian Large's BBC-TV production of 1975). This Wuppertal anachronism, incidentally, was inspired by a Herz production of 1962 in East Berlin.

Any opera-goer can supply his own ghastly examples of what Professor Nagler called "directional arrogance". Among my own favourites have been Friedrich's staging of *Der Freischütz* for the Royal Opera in 1977, interpreting

Weber's and Kind's decision to place the story at the time of the Thirty Years War as a prophetic vision of Vietnam, and giving us, accordingly, a defoliated Bohemia, a devastated countryside and a community rent by topical class warfare. Defoliation? Defloration, rather – of Weber and Kind – and of a treasurable masterpiece!

That, of course, was polemics again. But there was nothing polemical about Friedrich's showing us Siegfried in his Royal Opera *Götterdämmerung* (1976) paddling down the Rhine, reminding Americans in the audience of Hiawatha paddling down the Mississippi. If there was polemical intent in his having Alberich and Mime, in *Das Rheingold*, appear in minstrel-show blackface, presenting the giants as spacemen armed with ray guns and Freia as a well-padded Mae West, I missed the message.

Nor were there polemics in Peter Wood's *Die Entführung aus dem Serail* at Glyndebourne (1980), which proceeded from a conviction that the opera is about cages, and so gave us cages, lots of them, full of live doves, a birdseller flogging his birds to Selim Bassa during Konstanze's "Martern aller Arten" and Selim releasing a caged dove at the final curtain.

Social commentary of a kind – or correction – was the intention of Jonathan Miller's *The Marriage of Figaro* at the English National Opera in 1978, which had the Countess and Susanna wearing more or less identical clothes and wigs, and endowing the Countess with two children and a nanny. This was the same Jonathan Miller, by the way, who felt called upon in a later ENO *Othello* to soften Shakespeare's Elizabethan racism by giving us a whitish Moor, a swarthy Iago and a brunette Desdemona.

I could not imagine at the time (1977) what had inspired Peter Hall, in his Glyndebourne *Don Giovanni*, to put everyone under umbrellas. I heard subsequently that it was a jocular reference to rainy picnics in the Glyndebourne gardens. Not a good joke, and at Mozart's expense a bad one.

Nor could I fathom Elijah Moshinsky's reasoning in leaving Lohengrin up the Scheldt without a swan in his Royal Opera *Lohengrin* (1977) or the banquet without tables, victuals or drink in his Royal Opera *Macbeth* (1981).

Since then (1983) we have had David Pountney at the English National Opera setting Dvorak's *Rusalka*, that most sylvan of operas, in a child's nursery (the opera, we were told, is about adolescence), with our eponymous heroine addressing the moon from a swing. Next to her bed (more like an oversized crib) was a tiny ornamental pool. The Water Sprite was grandpa, rolling around in a wheel chair. A majority of critics, sad to relate, liked it.

They did not like – and there I was with them – an Ian Judge production of Gounod's *Faust*, also at the ENO (1985), which made a red-wigged tart out of Marguerite, and had her die not in prison, but in a lunatic asylum. Two supernumeraries were required to carry the jewel-box. While singing the Jewel Song, reclining, lingerie-clad, on luxurious scatter cushions in a palace garden dotted with statuary ("Salut demeure, chaste et pure"?), Marguerite admired herself in enormous mirrors held up and twirled by a bevy of half-naked Nubian myrmidons.

The ENO has favoured us with many another equally fanciful and equally offensive aberration: *Carmen* set in an automobile graveyard somewhere in Latin America (Pountney); *Tosca* and *Rienzi* set in Mussolini's Rome (Jonathan Miller and Nicholas Hytner); *Mazeppa* set in what appeared to be a gym used as a torture chamber (David Alden); *Cavalleria rusticana* and *Pagliacci* wedded and set in a British colliery town (Ian Judge); *Rigoletto* set in New York's Little Italy with the duke as a mafia princeling (Jonathan Miller); *The Valkyrie* and *The Magic Flute* both set in a library (Pountney and Miller); *Simon Boccanegra* in which Amelia made her entrance being dumped from her coffin at the close of the Prologue (Alden, again), and a Pountney *Queen of Spades* presented – as one critic put it – as "a nutter's nightmare."

Hytner's *Rienzi* (1983) deserves a paragraph to itself. Rienzi was represented as a 20th-century totalitarian, and the pageantry supplied by archive film clips of mass rallies and new film clips made to look like archive material showing Rienzi holding forth à la Mussolini, Hitler, *et al*. At the end, Rienzi and his cronies were gunned down by counter-revolutionaries reinforced by tanks, headlights blazing, etc.

Before leaving the ENO, a word for the Joachim Herz *Parsifal* of 1986. Herz gave us a Titural (properly an offstage voice) in person and the outcast Klingsor not in the turret of his castle, but flying about on a swing. The floor of his "castle" looked like a gigantic pizza, from which Kundry eventually emerged like a chunk of garlic rising to the surface. Its rim was raised to reveal Kundry's garden with a bevy of females looking more bathing beauty than floral. The forest surrounding Montsalvat looked to one perspicacious critic like "the intestines of Amfortas, or, possibly, what passed through them."

If I seem to have focused, thus far, too closely on the ENO, it is simply because at the Coliseum this "innovative," "adventurous" approach to opera production is a matter of declared policy, and the misdemeanours inevitably more numerous, more spectacular and, in my view, often more spectacularly awful. The Royal Opera tends rather to traditional production, but it has not escaped the plague. I have touched on Friedrich's *Ring* and *Der Freischütz* and Moshinsky's *Lohengrin* and *Macbeth*. More recently we have been exposed to a Mike Ashman *Der fliegende Holländer*, a Bill Bryden *Parsifal* and an Andrei Serban *Fidelio*, the latter ending with cardboard cut-out angels and devils on stilts.

The trouble in Ashman's *Holländer* began when we were introduced to Daland's home and the spinning room. Suddenly we were pitched forward to *c.* 1940 and what appeared to be a hawser factory with the women's chorus, white-smocked and mob-capped, presided over imperiously by Senta's nanny, Mary, from a high desk on rollers, and with a trousered Senta mooning over a portrait of the Dutchman in an attitude reminiscent of Salome drooling over the severed head of John the Baptist. Not a spinning wheel in sight, nor a stick of household furniture, making a mockery of the wonderfully onomatopoetic music Wagner devised for his spinning chorus.

The London critics had a lot of more or less innocent fun with Bryden's *Parsifal* (1988). Most agreed that the time was the early 1940s and the setting either west country England or Ulster, although one opted for Dresden. The ritual was described as vaguely Masonic. All agreed that what we were offered was "a communal act of story telling," or "a kind of communal and plebian mystery play." As this involved having members of the community playing their parts in the vaulted ruins of the local cathedral, the results excited levity.

The flower maidens, for example, were "an unappetizing lot in their satin slips, nighties and baby-dolls," or "the local eurythmics group stripped down to their undies," or "a gaggle of garlanded ladies in their night dresses." Gurnemanz suggested nothing more than "an amiable, sweetly-smiling do-gooder" or "a Mr. Chips-like Gurnemanz." The grail was "of Cup Final size," and the magic garden "a couple of nets of used Kleenex tissues."

The mischief has not, of course, been confined to London. The Kupfer *Fidelio* for Welsh National Opera has been noted. We go now to Glasgow for a Graham Vick *Oberon* (1985), in which Oberon was represented as half-sustainer of the universe, Rezia and Fatima as secretaries in the American Embassy of an Islamic state held hostage by the Ayatollah and rescued not by Sir Huon of Bordeaux and Sherasmin, but by two test pilots, Hugh and Godfrey.

And finally to Opera North at Leeds and a Michael McCarthy production of *Fidelio* in which, according to Michael Kennedy in *The Times* (30 April, 1988), "Act II is just plain awful. Florestan is incarcerated, Rocco tells us, in the deepest dungeon in the prison. Not here. He has a chair on the roof with stunted shrubs around, and he looks hale and hearty on his meagre diet. Up to this point, costumes have been historical. For the final scene, the chorus appear in modern grey suits, double-breasted for the men, large white bows for the women. They all have identification cards pinned to their lapels as at a sales conference. Why? Don't ask me!"

No. The pestilence has not been confined to London, nor to Great Britain. It is world-wide. Thus far, as a resident of London, I have touched on only those productions that I have myself attended, except for those in Cardiff, Glasgow and Leeds. Now, going abroad, I shall be dependent on the reports of critic/correspondents for *Opera*, *Opera News*, the London *Times*, the *New York Times*, and the *International Herald Tribune*.

Where better to begin than with Bayreuth, where it all started with Wieland Wagner's revolutionary – but reverent – staging of his grandfather's music-dramas, commencing with the re-opening of the festival in 1951, and with Patrice Chéreau's 1976 centenary production of *Der Ring des Nibelungen*?

It was heartily booed at the premiere by staunch Wagnerites horrified at seeing Siegfried in a dinner jacket, the Rhine Maidens as tarts cavorting in tatty cocktail dresses in the spray of a sluice below a hydroelectric dam, Wotan in Goethean or Dickensian attire (but still toting that spear) and many other departures from Wagnerian script and tradition.

I was not at Bayreuth, but caught the ten successive Sunday evening BBC-TV telecasts of 1982–3, and duly reported to the *International Herald Tribune* (November 10, 1982) that the image springing immediately to mind at the news of the telecasts was: "*Dallas* on the Rhine," or, as Humphrey Burton, the BBC-TV presenter, put it, "A kind of cosmic *Upstairs, Downstairs*." What we saw made those anticipatory images seem more truly appropriate than facetious.

This updating in setting and dress made it all the easier to see Wotan as Jock Ewing, Fricka as Miss Ellie, Freia as Lucy and possibly even Siegfried as J.R., although certainly not so bright. There was a loss of grandeur, of course, in this bringing of mythology down to earth, but – I grant – a telling gain in intelligibility, enhanced on the small screen.

What we learned, as we observed these creatures in close-up, and eavesdropped on their conversation, was that what the *Ring* is all about, when all is said and done, is greed and sex. We always knew it, to be sure, but here we saw it all spelled out. Instead of Valhalla – Dallas!

Things have not improved at Bayreuth. In Götz Friedrich's 1982 production of *Parsifal* we had, according to Donal Henahan, senior critic of the *New York Times*:

"A Kundry dressed like Rudolph Valentino and acting in the same eye-popping manner. . . . The wounded Amfortas staggers under a cross supported by two friends, while other followers carry pillows in case he wishes to pause for a rest. Titurel appears on a screen for a closed circuit TV conference with his son. More humorously, at least, Klingsor's garden is an erector set with a platform from which he presides as a stage manager, cruelly shining a spotlight on the unfortunate Kundry and giving orders to his minions by microphone."

I am indebted to Henahan again for this account of Werner Herzog's 1987 Bayreuth *Lohengrin*; "Mr. Herzog, changing stylistic gear with a lurch, placed the marriage bed out of doors in an ice-coated Brabantian landscape on what seemed to be either a shag rug or a clump of frozen tundra. Handmaidens stripped Lohengrin and Elsa down to their underwear in preparation for the main event, but the newlyweds didn't seem to notice any chill. The bed sheets, strikingly in this otherwise bleak milieu, appeared to be made of gold, while the headboard consisted of a large swan that resembled an ice sculpture one might find at an especially fancy smorgasbord. . . . For his climactic trick, the director materialized a small boy representing Elsa's lost brother, Gottfried, out of the swan's body. . . . Elsa did not die in Gottfried's arms, but lived on, obviously to be further conspired against (*Lohengrin* II?) by the insidious Ortrud."

Not so far away, in Hamburg, as recently as 1988, Wagner's *Tristan und Isolde* was similarly abused by Ruth Berghaus (another of the East German offenders). As James Helme Sutcliffe reported to the *International Herald Tribune*, she and her designer, Hans Dieter Schaal, "set the opera evidently on a space ship with a background of stars and a periodically passing moon, with twenty-four crew members doing slow synchronized pushups under as many deck chairs. . . . Act II took place within the huge turbine of the ship, a bright planet gliding past the rear opening at intervals. . . . In Act III Tristan went to sleep in an aluminum dinghy from which Isolde began her 'Liebestod' while rowing on dry land."

At roughly the same time, Paris could applaud or boo a *Ring* at the Théâtre des Champs-Elysées, a co-production with Nice Opéra directed by Daniel Mesguich, proceeding, we were told by Charles Pitt in *Opera* (June, 1988), from an assumption that "the *Ring* is about the death (or twilight) of Italian opera, with Wotan/Wagner trying to create a new sort of lyric art and dying in the attempt, the whole production set in and around an opera house.

"In *Das Rheingold*," Pitt continued, "a subsiding facade is keeling over; *Die Walküre* shows the auditorium with Nothung stuck into a caryatid. Nibelheim is an early 19th century operatic workshop with artisans compelled to perform the many tasks (tailoring, shoemaking, armour, etc.) that go into operatic production. Alberich is making his own opera, somewhat different from Wotan's. Siegfried takes place on stage. There is no forge, but Siegfried creates a great fire, a real blaze of Mime's books and tailor's dummies, to reforge Nothung." Etc.

Among further aberrations, Pitt noted Rhine Maidens represented as sophisticated ladies seated on chairs in wedding dresses; an Act I of *Die Walküre* with twenty-three people on stage; godly participants seeming to be traveling actors, usually with a suitcase to hand, and, as a final touch:

"Mesguich cannot resist poking fun at what one might call the 'Old Ring': In *Das Rheingold* the Rhine is represented by a length of red cloth stretching across the entire stage, down which march the characters of the 'Old Ring' in their horned helmets, lances in hand. They are seen again as the curtain rises on the Prelude to *Die Walküre* awkwardly scuttling offstage, as if their services were no longer required. The gods who replace them are, of course, in modern dress."

As I noted earlier, referring to Friedrich's *Parsifal*, things have not improved at Bayreuth. They have got worse, as demonstrated in Harry Kupfer's 1988 *Ring*. Again I am indebted to London colleagues for accounts of what earned Kupfer his eagerly anticipated booing. According to David Cairns in the *Sunday Times*:

"This *Ring* reached its conclusion in spectacular disaster not only for Wagner's gods. While some kind of nuclear catastrophe appeared to engulf the men and women standing round Siegfried's bier, and the huge projections of night-time New York which lined both sides of the Gibichung hall lurched and plummeted, other groups stood unscathed in front of the television screens apparently watching the event (or was it, as someone suggested, a video of the Chéreau *Ring*?)."

"For *Siegfried* Act I," Nicholas Kenyon told us in *The Observer*, "Mime has made his forge in a huge piece of discarded tubing thrown into the forest. In Act II we are in some structure of reinforced concrete which has been violently rent asunder, full of exposed wires and crushed tubes, with only a glimpse of the 'frische Wald' beyond. The dragon is, of course, a creation of tentacled tubing. In such grim ecological conditions a free woodbird seems improbable, so this one is produced by Wotan from his pocket and controlled by his spear – which rather overestimates his grip on the proceedings, but Kupfer is anxious to keep him involved far longer than Wagner was."

Verdi is no more immune than Wagner. Andrew Clark told us in *Opera* (April, 1988) of a production of *Falstaff* in Basel by Jean-Claude Auvray set in Verdi's Casa di Riposa in Milan: "Throughout the performance, the lines were blurred between an ageing, white-haired Verdi figure silently stalking the stage and Sir John Falstaff, bed-ridden, geriatric invalid-in-a-wheelchair and fat knight rolled into one. Ford, Caius, Bardolph and Pistol donned their operatic guises by divesting themselves of white medical overalls in which they attended the bed of the ailing composer. . . . Was it fair to print the standard synopsis in the programme book, and then expect everyone to understand why Falstaff's surroundings were those of an old folks' home rather than the Garter Inn?" No *riposa* for Verdi.

Or for Puccini, either. *Opera* of March, 1988, brought us an account by Alfred Frankenstein of a *La Bohème* at the Tel-Aviv Chamber Theatre in Israel:

"The success of the performance was regrettably reduced by the American producer David Alden's staging. He declared in an interview that he wanted to expel all the romanticism from Puccini and to change the 'bohemians' into hippies and beatniks. Unfortunately, he succeeded only too well. The four friends had to live on the roof in the open with no furniture except for a single chair they climbed from time to time. Act II ended not with Alcindoro fainting at the sight of the café bills given him, but with Colline drawing a revolver and shooting him: such is modern opera staging."

Still with Puccini and with the March, 1988, issue of *Opera* – and still with *La Bohème* – we heard from Rolf Fath of a production by Giancarlo del Monaco in Karlsruhe that "Rodolfo's typewriter, Alcindoro's convertible, in which he drove Musetta, and the belching factory chimneys at the Barrière d'enfer were subtly picturesque reminders of a fully developed industrialism."

The March, 1988, issue of *Opera* was truly a chamber of horrors. In addition to the above, we heard from Eduardo Arnosi in Buenos Aires that "No doubt the obsession with vengeance bordering on madness as reflected in Strauss's orchestra led Roberto Oswald to set his new production of *Elektra* in a mental hospital about 1915. . . . The surprise was that Orestes wore a straitjacket (when he eventually appeared), not Elektra."

That same issue also had Charles Pitt, again, from Paris telling us of a Göran Jarvefelt production of *Don Giovanni* at the Opéra-Comique that started out with Don Giovanni fleeing down a ladder, trousers in hand. Well, that was nothing. Jonathan Miller, at the Coliseum, had him dashing out of the house with no trousers at all. But when it comes to defacing *Don Giovanni* all other mayhem fades against Peter Sellars's production for the Summerfare Festival in Purchase, New York. Donal Henahan's notice in the *New York Times* began thus:

"You remember Mozart's *Don Giovanni*? That's the opera in which Don Juan of the slums interrupts the Champagne Aria to take a heroin hit in the arm from his pimp and connection, Leporello. Donna Anna also requires a quick needle during her 'Non mi dir' before she can launch into the coloratura section of that aria. Elvira, a Madonna clone, rolls back and forth across the stage like a bowling ball while making a hash of 'Mi tradì.' And you certainly will recall how Giovanni sits on a stoop outside a slum building in what may be Spanish Harlem, enjoying his last supper (a Big Mac and fries) as a big-box radio pumps out those great 18th century dance tunes. That, of course, leads up to the famous 'Stoned Guest' scene in which the dissolute Don is pulled down into a sewer by a small girl playing Lolita to his Humbert Humbert. . . .

"Evidently operating under the assumption that this 200 year-old work cannot speak to a modern audience unless it is trashed, trivialized and sensationalized, Mr. Sellars turns it into a depressing parade of easy jokes and vaudeville turns. During Leporello's Catalogue Aria, the Don's conquests are illustrated by a series of pornographic photos flashed on a screen, making it rather difficult to pay much attention to the singing. In burlesque, when all jokes failed, the comedian traditionally resorted to dropping his pants; here, Don Giovanni and his pals periodically strip and dance about in jockey shorts. In the finale, enigmatically, other principals turn nudist and pop out of holes in the stage to celebrate the victory of good over evil."

Would it be superfluous to add that the same Peter Sellars also favored Summerfare with a production of *Così fan tutte* set in Despina's diner?

The root of all this presumptuous, arrogant and often licentious mischief is the crisis of opera in this century, i.e., the stagnation of the repertoire and the scarcity of truly great singers. Opera houses – like concert halls – have become museums, but unlike other museums, their artefacts cannot be preserved for exhibition from walls in galleries or storing on the shelves of public and private libraries. They have to be animated continually in performance by musicians –

conductors, instrumentalists, vocalists, dancers and choreographers and, in the case of opera, by stage directors and their designers.

Instead, however, of accepting museum status and identity as a fact of life, and administering their museums with a proper regard for the care, maintenance and exhibition of their treasures – as those responsible for concerts, oratorio and recitals mostly do – the directors of opera houses all over the world have clung naively, tenaciously and desperately to the illusion that opera is still a living contemporary art. Granted, those responsible for concerts, oratorios and recitals cultivate an illusion of vitality, continuity and validity by commissioning and performing new music that few other than a handful of hopeful critics wish to hear. But in the presentation of their treasure of inherited masterpieces and near-masterpieces, they are, if anything, even too solicitous of traditional identity, character and performance practice. Not so on the part of those responsible for the preservation and presentation of opera treasure.

Unable to update the music, which in opera, too, is solicitously treated, they have looked to a new breed of producer, mostly from theater and film, to sustain the illusion of vitality and continuity by updating and altering the staging in cynical violation of tradition and oblivious of, or indifferent to, the consequent stylistic anachronisms, aberrations, abominations and – not to mince words about it – vandalism. Much of what we have seen in the past thirty years, as illustrated in the examples I have cited, reflects about as much taste, appreciation, insight and respect for a work of art as painting a Dali moustache on the Mona Lisa or adding art deco accessories to a Sheraton sideboard.

One hears it argued that all this is necessary if opera is to be made accessible, intelligible and "relevant" to a widening, unsophisticated and predominantly young audience, many of them being exposed to these operas – or to any opera – for the first time. The counter-argument, to which I subscribe, is that if operas cannot be made acceptable and attractive to a wider audience on their own merits and on their composers' and librettists' own terms, they should not be given at all, or else directed to, and tailored for, a smaller, more responsibly receptive audience. There is, after all, limitless variation and refinement open to the imaginative producer, stage director or designer within the dramatic, graphic and period framework suggested or prescribed by a work's authors.

The harm, even evil, in the present fashionable approach and procedure is not done to someone like me, who has been an opera buff in America and

Europe for more than sixty years. It is done to the young newcomer. If he is led to believe, after attendance at a *Cavalleria rusticana* and *Pagliacci* set in a British colliery town and sung in English, that he has experienced Mascagni's *Cavalleria rusticana* and Leoncavallo's *Pagliacci*, he is being wilfully deceived. Ditto for a *Carmen* set in a 20th-century Latin American automobile graveyard, and so on through scores of operas more or less recently exposed to the produceritis or conceptitis virus. Sir Peter Hall put it cogently in a BBC-2 interview (2 June, 1988):

"I wouldn't want any child of mine to see Jonathan Miller's 'Mafia' version of *Rigoletto* as a first experience of Verdi's opera. It's OK, but it's not *Rigoletto*. It's a comment on *Rigoletto*. It limits a great work by exploring a very small corner of it. It's like doing *Hamlet* in plus-fours, or producing *The Tempest* as an anti-colonial play. It's too easy. A great opera production is a quintessence of theatre."

What has happened is that, under the mask of "innovation" and "adventure", and in quest of a wider audience, opera houses all over the world have been going down-market, appealing to the innocently impressionable and gullible. It constitutes an affront not only to the art of composers and librettists – all dead and incapable of self-defence – but also to cultivated audiences.

Characteristic of almost all contemporary opera production is an assumption on the part of the producer that what we have in the form of an accepted musical and theatrical masterpiece is insufficient unto itself and its audience. The music and the composer's or librettist's stage directions can no longer be counted on to make their effect without visual and interpretive assistance. What is implicit and often wonderfully graphic in the music must be made explicit on the stage. And so we have the curtain up and activity of some sort during the playing of an overture or instrumental interlude. There must be visual diversion during the singing of an aria or concerted number lest the audience's attention flag. It is, I believe, significant that so many of these producers have first made their name in the theater or film or TV rather than in the opera house. They don't trust the music.

What happens most of the time is that the producer gets in the composer's way and diverts the audience's attention from the composer's accomplishment, a procedure aptly termed "fashionably obtrusive" by Robert Henderson, reviewing Kupfer's appalling new production of *Pelléas et Mélisande* for the English National Opera (1981) in the *Daily Telegraph*. It is a curious and hilarious paradox that in concert, oratorio and recital in these same thirty or so years the trend has been in the precisely opposite direction; toward stylistic authenticity and minute observation of the performance practices and conventions prevailing at the time of a work's origin!

Reaction and reform are long overdue, and they will be resisted, as demonstrated in the Christmas issue of *About the House*, the magazine of The Friends of Covent Garden (1981), where we found Elizabeth Forbes holding forth at length on both Nagler and the *Daily Telegraph* (for its Marx brothers leader) in an article titled "Anti-Anti". Reading this article, in total disagreement, of course, left me grateful to Miss Forbes for having provided, from her extensive experience of contemporary German opera productions, much welcome and even amusing support for my own singly "anti" position. Most treasurable, perhaps, was her glowing account of a Hans Neuenfels production of *Aida* in Frankfurt two seasons earlier.

Neuenfels, she told us, "most controversial and most exciting of today's German producers, takes a bifocal view of *Aida*, from the perspective of the 1870s and the 1980s, contemporary with Verdi and contemporary with himself and his audience. Archeologist-Radames addresses 'Celeste Aida' to a statue he has unearthed, but what he is really digging up is 19th century opera, a salutary reminder, perhaps, that so much operatic production has ossified in that period. Aida herself scrubs the floors of the museum – another dig at the petrification of opera as an art form – while chorus-spectators of 1871 or 1872 laugh at the ballet of African 'savages' much as the Parisian audience laughed at *Tannhäuser* a decade later [sic]."

More recently (*Opera*, April, 1988), we have had Geoffrey Wheatcroft taken to task by a majority of correspondents for an article entitled briefly and forthrightly: "It's Got To Stop" (February, 1988). Wheatcroft, it is pertinent to note, is not a professional music critic. He was at the time a columnist for the *Sunday Telegraph*. It was not the kind of article one would expect from the professional critics. They are, whether they acknowledge it or not, associated with the Establishment and with Virgil Thomson's "conspiracy to defend the faith." They feel free to like or dislike this or that production, but not to attack produceritis as the plague that it is.

What inspired Wheatcroft's splendid polemic was a production of *Die Walküre* at the Grand Théatre in Geneva by the Norwegian Stein Winge, in which:

"Through the gloom of the stage picture can be seen a male figure upstage, shackled to what might be a tree trunk in the posture traditionally associated with St. Sebastian. What is he doing there? What, for that matter, is this drapery of fish-nets illuminated by searchlights meant to suggest? Where are we? The answer comes before long: 'Dies Haus und dies Weib sind Hundings eigen.'

"With Hunding himself there enters a squad of soldiers in fatigues. What are *they* doing? An explanation of sorts emerges after Hunding's recognition of Siegmund and his threat of vengeance at 'Zur Rache ward ich gerufen, Sühne zu nehmen für Sippenblut.' The squaddies cut down the shackled figure (a Wälsung hostage, are we to suppose?), bring him downstage, and then ceremoniously cut his throat.

"His [Winge's] further innovations included a huge bank of flickering television screens onstage (bring back surtitles, thought I, or nearly) and the setting of the opening of Act II in an art deco bathroom where Wotan wallows in the jacuzzi as Fricka mixes his cocktail."

More recently we have read (*Opera*, November, 1988) of a *Der fliegende Höllander* staged by Jean-Claude Auvray, in which Rolf Fath told us, "Senta does not work up gradually to her pathological obsessions, but is from the outset a patient in a secure institution where her great emotional outbursts are restrained by confinement in a straitjacket."

I missed David Pountney's new *La traviata* for the English National Opera at the Coliseum (September, 1988), and so am indebted to John Higgins in *The Times* (19 September), for this account of the setting and what happened at the end of Act I:

"Apparently the Parisian roué's ideal vision in the middle of the last century was a blonde in her underwear amidst a field of ripening corn with a useful red plush *chaise-longue* to hand. This platform of corn arises in the middle of the dining tables during the soirée. Helen Field's Violetta, the image in question, has to sing the act's closing scene in heavily corseted *déshabillé* after her jaded guests have tossed in some payment for their evening's entertainment, just as satisfied spectators in the same era might throw coins into the ring at the end of a prize fight. You may call it a Victorian *East of Eden*. But it is exceedingly difficult to call it *La traviata*".

Higgin's notice was headed, appropriately, "Corn, Soft Porn and Poppycock," and he closed it with this sobering reflection:

"Perhaps this *Traviata* poses a larger question beyond the immediate failure of the staging. ENO has a truly deserved reputation for innovation, especially of production and design. But it is also acquiring a less enviable one for perverse interpretation of some of the cornerstones of the repertoire. With probably more of the first-time audience for a *Traviata* or a *Carmen* coming to the Coliseum than to any other British theatre, that should cause some worries."

From New York we hear from C.J. Luten, in *Opera News* (December, 1988), that Peter Sellars, having staged *Così fan tutte* in Despina's diner and *Don Giovanni* in New York's Spanish Harlem, has rounded off the Mozart-Da Ponte trio with a *Le nozze di Figaro* set in Manhattan's Trump Tower (52nd floor).

And from Los Angeles we hear from Paul Moor in *The Times* of an autumn, 1988, production by David Alden of *Wozzeck* in which "Georg Büchner's wretched soldier wears the camouflage combat garb of the US Army, complete with the green beret unequivocally associated with Vietnam. His girl Marie, turned here into a boozy, barefoot slattern in short, basic black, occupies a vast room furnished entirely with a baby carriage, an easy chair and an electric washing machine."

Finally (for the moment) to Hamburg and a Peter Palitzsch production of *Fidelio* where, according to Sutcliffe in the *International Herald Tribune*, "The sublime Act I 'canonic' quartet was sung while its participants consumed soup in Rocco's ghastly pink kitchen. Leonore's 'Abscheulicher!' had to be delivered as she picked her way downstage between the ties of a blue neon railway track. And as all dramatic producers assume that opera audiences are particularly dull witted, she had to strip off her uniform jacket to prove that she was really a bosomy lady, not the youth Fidelio we had thought her to be. And why was Florestan shown – crimson-robed Rocco and Leonore on either side – as a crucifixion tableau in Dürer style? Poor Josef Protschka sang the cruel tessitura with breathtaking ease, but as his Florestan was taped to a cross and clothed only in a loincloth, nobody listened."

And so on and on and on.

What to do about it?

Send in the clowns?

With apologies to Stephen Sondheim: "Don't bother. They're here!"

4

Ordeal by (Tele)Vision

MANY, many years ago, when John Foster Dulles, as President Eisenhower's Secretary of State, was establishing a precedent for jet-propelled statesmanship and diplomacy, an article on his peripatetic predilections by James Reston, political correspondent of the *New York Times*, appeared in the *International Herald Tribune* under the heading: 'Don't just *do* something, Foster. *Stand* there!'

I have been reminded of that sobering admonition time and again while watching video broadcasts of operas with a rising gorge. I hasten to add that it is not just televised opera that prompts me to shout those words at the invisible producer and director. I am similarly aroused, and have been for many years, by almost all telecasts of musical events – symphony concerts, chamber music, recitals, oratorios, etc.

I turn on my TV set in happy anticipation of an opera or an oratorio or a symphony concert to be savoured in the comfort and convenience of my living room, and within ten minutes find myself covering my eyes with my hands and wishing producer and director a nasty sojourn in a purgatory where they will be required to spend eighteen hours a day exposed to the horrors of their own mischief. I am speaking of televised performances, not of documentaries.

What makes these people think that we need to be shown, in microscopic close-up, what horns, oboes, flutes, clarinets, trumpets, fiddles, trombones, double basses and timpani – and their players – look like? What makes them think that we need – or want – a guided tour of the orchestra, and right in the middle of a performance?

What makes them think that appreciation – or enjoyment – is enhanced by isolating a soloist or a section visually from all that is going on about them, thus distorting the relationship of soloist or section and ensemble? What makes them think that the listener or viewer gains anything from close-ups of sopranos, altos, tenors and basses, section by section, during the performance of an oratorio or any other choral work?

What makes them think that the enjoyment of opera is assisted by an examination of a prima donna's molars or the mole on her cheek or the agitation of her tongue and soft palate? What makes them think that the performance of sacred music profits from a survey of icons and stained glass windows, diverting our attention from what is being played and sung?

I was delighted and reassured, in a letter to *Musical Times* (June, 1988) from Robert Donington (quoted elsewhere in these pages on the subject of unwritten appoggiaturas), to find myself not alone in my annoyance and anger at this artistically destructive misuse and misapplication of cinematic technology.

"There are great benefits to be had," Donington wrote, "from the televising of opera – that I cannot for one moment doubt. But there are also considerable hazards, and the inconsiderate use of close-ups is surely one of them. Recently I was watching the live television broadcast of *Ariadne* from the New York Met, and a very well-conceived production in the main it seemed to be. But the camera team's tricks with their astonishing lenses played havoc with the experience. Jessye Norman was giving a technically and musically magnificent performance in this dramatically somewhat problematic role, and half the time she was being brought so close, with her vocal apparatus all too visibly at work and her mouth (naturally) open, that she might almost as well have been doing a commercial for toothpaste. I write this savagely, because I feel savagely. It was simply not fair. She is a lovely singer and a very good actress, but her chances of projecting this archetypal Ariadne were very largely dissipated through no fault of her own."

For my own part, I am reluctant to cite examples, if only because the malaise among producers and directors is so pervasive that it would be unjust to single out one or two culprits when so many are equally guilty. There are always at least a half dozen more or less mobile cameras capable of variable proximity to the target, with a monitor presiding over continual shifting from one distance, angle, focus or close-up to another, so that the viewer's eye is incessantly diverted from the preoccupation of the ear.

The reason for all this cinematic restlessness is, I have been told by some of those responsible, anxiety lest the listener or viewer's attention flag if not continuously stimulated by a new picture, a new camera angle, etc. Another reason, I suspect, although no one has told me so, is that if you have all those cameras and their crews you are expected to do something with them, that as producer or director you are supposed to *do* something, regardless of the fact that, having set the stage, the cameras and the lighting, the best thing to do is nothing. Again I find a kindred spirit in Robert Donington. At the close of his letter to *Musical Times* he wrote:

"I recall some five years back a telecast of *Idomeneo*, also from the New York Met, where the cameras seemed to have settled down more or less in the front row of the dress circle, and the degree of zooming in and panning around was so moderate and intelligent that it positively enhanced the experience without confusing it. The techniques can work, but only if they are used with a clear understanding of what opera itself is all about. Not too close, and not too often is about the size of it."

I agree. The root of the evil lies, I think, in the failure of producers and directors to grasp or acknowledge the importance to the masterpieces of European music of at least an impression of the spatial setting for which they were conceived. Even more fundamental is the failure to acknowledge the essential character of these masterpieces, including especially opera, as *aural, musical* experience.

Geoffrey Wheatcroft, in his "It's Got to Stop" article, cited earlier, went to the heart of the matter when he wrote:

"It is a commonplace that opera has moved in the past century and a half through three ages: those of the singer, of the conductor and of the producer. As a personal foible, I imagine that the second would have been the happiest to live through (most music lovers, not always the same as opera-goers, would, I think, agree), and that the last is in many ways the worst. Whatever they may have inflicted on opera, the singer and conductor were, at least, musicians. They could not have been guilty of the ultimate heresy of supposing that opera is anything other than a musical art form."

True, and to the point, but it is not "purely" or "exclusively" a musical form, which several of *Opera*'s irate correspondents accused him – inaccurately, incorrectly and falsely – of asserting. It embraces the theatrical, the visual and the literary. But what distinguishes it from other art forms is that it is – or should be – a *predominantly* musical form, and that, as such, the predominant element is – or should be – the voice raised and sustained in song.

This is something the composers, librettists and lyricists of the American musical never forgot, which is why the musical prospered at just the time when contemporary European opera was fading because that truth had been forgotten. When operas are filmed or televised, a new element is added, and it is a vital one: space.

Operas, concerts, oratorios and recitals are, to be sure, *seen* in the opera house, concert hall, church or recital room. But they are seen from a distance, and the distance is constant. There is no shifting of the listener's position to change the angle of vision or the point of view. On record, of course, they are not even seen.

What TV and film producers and directors do with their restless camera work, close-ups and other visual distractions – worse, as a rule, in studio productions than in the filming of live stage performances – diverts the listener's or viewer's attention from composition, performance and performer, thus working precisely against the objectives of composer and performer, sometimes by over-concentration on the individual singer at the expense of the singer's theatrical context and environment, sometimes by shifting attention away from the singer in mid-aria, as if the director were afraid that the viewer's concentration span may not stay the course. Producers of opera in the opera house often proceed in a similar fashion, but on film the diversion is grossly magnified and even more disastrous.

I have sometimes been tempted to think that these people hate music. In a more temperate frame of mind I doubt it. But of one thing, on the evidence of what I see on my TV screen month after month, I am certain: music scares the hell out of them!

5

Evviva l'Appoggiatura!

"Giunse alfin il momento . . ." I shall translate it as "The moment has at last arrived," and hope that the next time I hear a Susanna sing it, in Italian, of course, including the recitative that leads into "Deh! vieni no tardar" in the last act of Mozart's *Le nozze di Figaro* I shall hear the unwritten appoggiatura on the *men* of "momento."

The moment for what? The moment to come to grips with one of the most vexatious and exasperating infelicities in the performance of Mozart's operas as they have come to us in opera houses all over the world and on record for the better part of this declining century – and not only Mozart's.

It arises from the question or problem of unwritten ornamentation, most specifically and conspicuously from the question of what to do about the habit, practice or convention common to composers of the baroque era of ending phrases of cadences, in both recitatives and arias, weakly and inarticulately on two identical notes when the most rudimentary musicality or feeling for the lyrical contours of speech cries out for an appoggiatura.

For the sake of simplicity and intelligibility let us stay, for the time being, with Mozart, acknowledging that what applies to his operas and other vocal music applies also to just about everything written for the solo singer from Handel's time and earlier to Beethoven (*Fidelio*) and even Rossini and Weber.

The Italian *appoggiare* means, according to the dictionaries, to lean, to rest, to back up, to support. In vocal music, and in instrumental music, too, the appoggiatura serves to give eloquence, elegance and pathos to a cadence or phrase ending, to give emphasis to declamatory utterance and so on, in short to achieve a lyrical extension of the emphases and cadences of speech.

Our problem lies in the fact that composers and singers in the baroque era understood this so well that composers did not bother to write in the appoggiaturas. Since other devices were available to enhance a cadence or a particular turn of melodic phrase, composers, as we shall see, settled for a code which left the executant's options open, but certainly did not invite or condone the omission of the elementary appoggiatura.

48

We can return now to Susanna for a typical example of the code, or composer shorthand:

a

b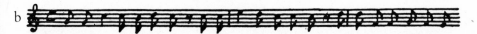

In these examples, (a) is what appears in the score, (b) shows how Mozart's Susanna would have read it and sung it. Just sing the two versions to yourself, and you will not have to consult a musicologist or conductor to accept (b) as the more eloquent, the more musical of the two.

After the baroque era composers began to leave less to the singer's discretion, prompted by exasperation and impatience with indiscretion, and to write the appoggiaturas into the notation. But they did not immediately deny the singer the prerogative of introducing them elsewhere when deemed appropriate by the singer, as documented as late as 1851 in what Verdi wrote over Rigoletto's conspiring with Sparafucile in Act III following the quartet: "Questo recitativo dovrà essere detto senza le *solite* appoggiature" – This recitative is to be given without the *customary* appoggiaturas (italics added).

The convention of the cadence ending on two identical notes appears hundreds, even thousands of times in Mozart's operas and concert arias and in those of other composers of the baroque era. The common reasoning offered by those who insist that the cadences be sung as written is: "If the composer had wanted the appoggiaturas, he would have written them." Modern musicology (as well as musical common sense) disagrees.

Robert Donington, in his article on Ornaments in *New Grove*, writes of "Unwritten Appoggiaturas": "Often the performer may or indeed should add an appoggiatura of appropriate duration even when there is no indication or sign in the written text. Both Quantz and C.P.E. Bach gave hints for recognizing such a situation, and both stressed the absolute necessity of adding an appoggiatura in certain instances. . . .

"There is one special case in which a convention of notation used throughout the 18th century necessitates an appoggiatura that is very far from obvious in the written text: in baroque recitatives many cadences, whether passing or final, appear to end on two repeated notes (so written to indicate to the accompanist the final harmony) that are actually intended to be executed

49

as an appoggiatura and its resolution. . . . The baroque acceptance of an appoggiatura in this awkward situation indicates how unstylish it would be for a modern performer to omit it."

In his *A Performer's Guide to Baroque Music* (1973), Donington is even more exacting: "Appoggiaturas in later baroque recitative are obligatory (a) to fill in a cadential interval of a (descending) third; (b) to diversify a feminine (and sometimes masculine) ending, even with no such third to fill in." As to "feminine" and "masculine", Donington explains: "It is easy to remember that a masculine cadence has the rhythm: 'I am a man' and that a feminine cadence has the rhythm: 'I am a woman.'" Susanna, in beginning her recitative, gives an example of a feminine cadence, which, according to Donington, "has the stronger claim to be given an appoggiatura."

The Viennese pianist and musicologist, Paul Badura-Skoda, in his *Mozart-Interpretation* (1957), is similarly specific and peremptory: "Vocal appoggiaturas are appoggiaturas which, according to a tradition observed far into the 19th century, are without exception to be sung differently than notated," and he cites in support Bernhard Paumgartner (1887–1971), Austrian musicologist, composer and conductor and longtime director of the Salzburg Mozarteum (1917–38, 1949–59), in *Musikerziehung*, vol. 4, pp. 229:

"With Mozart, in recitatives, arias [!] and ensembles, the introduction of the appoggiatura must be regarded as absolutely indispensable. . . . With Mozart there are many classical passages where the non-introduction of the vocal appoggiatura must be regarded as a crude violation of the style of this music. In Mozart's time – and long before and long afterwards – the appoggiatura was far more generously employed than even today's most ardent appoggiatura enthusiast would dare to assume."

When preparing this essay for publication in *About the House*, magazine of The Friends of Covent Garden (December 1986), I was unaware that Sir Charles Mackerras had written two excellent articles in a similar vein more than twenty years earlier (for *Opera*, October 1963, and *Records and Recording*, February 1965). They have been reprinted as an appendix to Nancy Phelan's biography of Sir Charles (1987), and I draw upon them gratefully for sources that escaped my survey, or were overlooked, notably Domenico Corri (1746–1825), Manuel Garcia (1805–1906), Peter Lichtenthal (1788–1853), Giambattista Mancini (1714–1800) and Vincenzo Manfredini (1737–99).

From Corri, who was a pupil of Porpora, and thus an older contemporary of Mozart (he emigrated first to Edinburgh, then to London, establishing a notable reputation as teacher, impresario, publisher and composer), we hear:

"We do find our mode of noting not only deficient, but erroneous, for . . . such a mode of noting has been used as might necessarily lead the singer, if guided by it alone, into positive error. . . . Indeed, either an air or a recitative sung exactly as it is commonly noted, would be a very inexpressive, nay uncouth performance; for not only the respective duration of the notes is scarcely hinted at, but one note is frequently marked instead of another, as is the case when a note is repeated instead of that note with its proper appoggiatura or grace . . . in consequence of which the singer is misled by being made to sing a wrong note."

From Garcia, son of Rossini's first Almaviva, brother of Maria Malibran and Pauline Viardot, and the 19th century's most eminent vocal pedagogue, in his *Traité de l'art du chant* (1847): "Two repeated notes followed by a rest are never sung as written. In the serious recitative, just as in those of comic nature, the necessity of accentuation demands that one change the first of the two notes into an appoggiatura, from above or below, according to the dictates of good taste. . . . In Italian vocal music, the appoggiatura *can hardly be considered an ornament, for it is required by the prosodic accent*" (italics added).

Mackerras quotes Lichtenthal from his *Dizionario* (1826): "The appoggiatura from above is the most frequently used ornament, and is indispensable in recitatives, such as the descending third. The Italian school has made the singers so familiar with these appoggiaturas that composers refrain from notating them in the recitatives."

And so to Mancini in his *Riflessioni pratiche sul canto* (1774): "All the excellence of the recitative depends on the knowledge of the proper use of the appoggiatura, or the musical accent, as it is generally called. This precious accent, in which is contained all the grace of a *cantilena*, consists, in short, of one note a tone higher than that written, and this is practiced especially when a word of several syllables is written with notes of the same pitch."

Finally to Manfredini in his *Regole armoniche* (1775): "Whereas an instrumentalist is not strictly required to perform appoggiaturas not indicated by the composer, this is not the same for the singer, who (especially in recitative) whenever he sees two notes of the same value and pitch, must consider the first of these as an appoggiatura from above; that is, particularly on a strong beat, he must perform it a tone or a semitone higher according to the key in which the notes are written."

Well, one can dispute historians, ancient commentators and musicologists, but what can the note-faithful offer against the explicit advice of one of the baroque era's most esteemed composers, Georg Philipp Telemann (1681–1767)? In a foreword to his *Harmonischer Gottesdienst* (1725), a set of cantatas for each Sunday and church festival, he advises the singer, in the recitatives, to "bear in mind that he should not always sing the notes as written, but from time to time make use of the so-called accents [appoggiaturas]." And he offers an example from the recitative of the first cantata, giving first the notes as written, then beneath them the notes 'more or less" as they should be sung.

It can be, and has been, argued that Telemann's evidence is suspect because of his belonging to an earlier generation than Mozart's. But Mozart, fortunately, left evidence of his own, if less explicitly didactic. Here, again, I am indebted to Sir Charles Mackerras, and it is pertinent to note that the evidence he cites is not in a recitative, but in an aria:

"Although Mozart never wrote any instructions on the use of appoggiaturas, we do find him carefully notating them whenever he wanted to show a particular singer the true method of interpretation. Here are parts of his aria, 'Non so d'onde viene' (K.294), as he wrote it first and as he embellished it later for his beloved Aloysia Weber. (The embellished autograph is in the City Archives, Braunschweig.) In the examples the original version appears above and Mozart's own performing version underneath. Every ending has an appoggiatura inserted":

In the face of such authoritative evidence of the essential nature and function of the appoggiatura at cadences ending on two identical notes or in a descending third – and we are dealing here with only its rudimentary and most obviously appropriate, even obligatory, employment (Telemann's example includes appoggiaturas applied in situations that go beyond the scope of this discussion) – one asks, inevitably, why the prejudice against it, as reflected in most performances of baroque vocal music throughout the greater part of this century. The obvious answer is honourably motivated and fashionable, but misguided, fidelity to the composer's text, and ignorance or dismissal of what is known of baroque performance practice and conventions, as well as a tendency to regard all tradition as an accretion incompatible with our contemporary taste and standards.

The most familiar and spectacular example of these attitudes is the policy adopted and imposed by Fritz Busch and Carl Ebert in the founding of the Glyndebourne Festival in 1934 by John Christie, reflected and documented in the famous recordings of *Le nozze di Figaro*, *Così fan tutte* and *Don Giovanni* of 1935 and 1936. The policy, and the fame and success of the recordings, were fatefully influential. For an account of what happened there we can draw upon Spike Hughes's historical essay for the programme book of the 50th anniversary Glyndebourne Festival of 1984:

"The second, almost general, criticism of the first Glyndebourne season was one that could be made annually until quite recently: the total elimination of all appoggiaturas. Busch and Ebert had made a point of avoiding what they called the 'velvet-and-chocolate' Mozart of Vienna, so perhaps no appoggiatur-as was a natural consequence. It would have been interesting to know whether

Busch thought Mahler's Mozart was 'velvet-and-chocolate', for he was famous during his ten years as director of the Vienna Opera for his insistence on appoggiaturas not only in Mozart, but also in Beethoven (*Fidelio*) and Weber, and his practice was followed by singers of the generation after his great Vienna ensemble (Elisabeth Schumann, for instance). No sooner did Mahler leave Vienna [in 1907], however, than his successor, Weingartner, promptly cut all appoggiaturas from everything. What was more surprising was that Bruno Walter, Mahler's most devoted disciple, also ignored Mozart's appoggiaturas."

I find most significant in the above the putative reasoning given for the prohibition of appoggiaturas, namely, that Busch and Ebert did not want the "velvet-and-chocolate" Mozart of Vienna. This would seem to suggest that they did not want a baroque Mozart, which strikes me as being the equivalent of seeking to improve on Austrian and Bavarian baroque churches by removing the decorations (making them "relevant" to 20th-century viewers?), and to be, indeed, even more reprehensible than the more familiar reasoning that "if Mozart had wanted them, he would have written them," which proceeds not from wilful and wanton violation of style, but from more or less innocent ignorance. Can we detect here an anticipation of the "relevant" mischief of today's opera producers?

Things have improved at Glyndebourne and elsewhere in the past decade, but not enough. What we hear suggests that some, if by no means all, conductors are content to leave the decision on whether or not to introduce appoggiaturas, at least in recitatives, up to the singers and their coaches, who are not sufficiently versed in the history of performance practice and convention to decide wisely. For guidance in such decision-making they need a Mackerras or an Erich Leinsdorf. The latter in his book, *The Composer's Advocate* (1981), is worth hearing on this subject:

"The tradition was to write out everything for the instruments, while treating the voice parts to a different spelling of the same cadential phrases. In the days of Beethoven and earlier, it could be assumed that singers knew the tradition and would amend the written parts accordingly in performance. . . . Beethoven, his contemporaries and their predecessors would have been astonished at the notion that personal preference had any bearing on a tradition so long accepted as that of the appoggiatura. Yet the unimaginative rigidity of musical training during most of the 19th century so firmly inculcated the idea that music must be played or sung exactly as written that centuries of tradition were nearly washed down the drain."

Or Mackerras: "Composers of the last 100 years or so have written their music exactly as it is to be performed, and conductors and repetiteurs all over the operatic world have drummed into singers that they are interpreting the composer's wishes only if they sing his works exactly as written. Performers are now so conditioned to this exactness that they tend to apply the principle to all music. Because Wagner, Strauss, Puccini and Britten wrote precisely, they expect the same of Mozart, Beethoven and Handel. Thus a number of unwritten traditions have become thrown out or forgotten.

"Conductors, anxious to expunge all the excessive ornamentation in which 19th century singers indulged, threw out the baby with the bath water, and got rid of the appoggiatura as well, forgetting that it is not just an optional embellishment, but forms an essential part of the melodic style of all vocal music of the 18th and early 19th centuries."

Both Leinsdorf and Mackerras might have noted that the relative standing of composer and singer in the baroque era and beyond was such that the convention of closing a cadence with two repeated notes may be seen as reflecting not only the composer's way of avoiding a *written* dissonance on an accented beat, but also a conventional deference to the singer. The appoggiatura was accepted as essential by both composer and singer, but the repeated note code gave the singer the option of elaborating it. When composers, including Mozart, wanted *only* the appoggiatura, they often wrote it in. How singers felt about the matter is pertinently and vividly revealed in Pier Francesco Tosi's outburst in his *Observations on the Florid Song* (1723) against composers who presumed to indicate appoggiaturas with a sign:

"If the scholar be well instructed in this, the appoggiaturas will become so familiar to him by continual practice that by the time he has come out of his first lessons he will laugh at those composers that mark them with a design, either to be thought modern or to show that they understand the art of singing better than the singers. . . . Poor Italy! Pray tell me: do not singers nowadays know where appoggiaturas are to be made unless they are pointed at with a finger?. . . . Oh, injurious insult to your modern singers who submit to instruction fit for children. Let us imitate foreigners in those things only wherein they excel!"

Those now active in investigating the performance practices of early music are handicapped by the fact that they have no recordings of Bach, Handel and Scarlatti actually playing to help in documenting their conclusions. They have only the written word of their contemporaries: C.P.E. Bach, Quantz, Rameau, etc. There are no recordings of Mozart and his singers, either. But in the case of Haydn, Mozart, Beethoven, Weber, Rossini, etc., we do have a wealth of recordings by singers who were far closer to the composer's time than we, and whose performance procedures may safely be assumed to reflect those of the composer's contemporaries. Fashion and taste in performance did not change so rapidly two centuries ago, or even a century ago, as they do today.

These old records by earlier singers, most of them past their prime at the time of recording, may not sound well, but they contain much information. The oldest singer in terms of year of birth audible on record or tape, and probably the first opera singer to be recorded (not commercially available), is the Danish bass-baritone Peter Schram (1819–1895), who in 1889 recorded on an Edison cylinder, without accompaniment and in Danish, Leporello's entrance aria and a fragment of Leporello's "Catalogue".

Not only are the appoggiaturas all there (with one exception, of which more later), but also a delightful turn (gruppetto) on the first syllable of the Danish equivalent of "*gal*antuomo" and a vocal flourish at the fermata following "ed io far la sentinella". Schram had been a student of Manuel Garcia in Paris in 1846, and Garcia had been with his father's company in New York when they gave the first American performances of *Don Giovanni* in Italian with the collaboration of none other than Lorenzo da Ponte.

Also a student of Garcia (a decade later in London) was Sir Charles Santley. He recorded Figaro's "Non più andrai" in 1903 at the age of 69, and there we hear the same procedure, including turns on "amoroso" and "girando" (suggested in Mozart's instrumental introduction) and another at the cadence on "poco cont*ante*". He, too, supplies a flourish, even more elaborate, at the fermata following the last "brillante". Like Schram, he omits one appoggiatura, and, as in Schram's case, it is the first of a sequence, omitted, presumably, to avoid repetitiveness.

From Lilli Lehmann (1848–1929) we have Donna Anna's "Or sai chi l'onore", recorded in 1905, with the appoggiaturas on "l'on*ore*" and "*v*olse" and at every other pertinent cadence. And from Johanna Gadski (1872–1932) we have Donna Elvira's "Mi tradì quell'alma in*grata*" with the appoggiaturas on "in*grata*" and its repetition and so on, including all the recitatives with every appoggiatura right where it belongs. This recording, incidentally, was made in Camden, New Jersey, in 1908 when Gadski was singing Donna Elvira at the Met under Mahler.

Especially treasurable – and instructive – are two recordings of the "La ci darem la mano" duet from *Don Giovanni,* the one with Mattia Battistini and Emilia Corsi, the other with Antonio Scotti and Geraldine Farrar. Both were made in the very early years of the century, and both observe the appoggiaturas in the introductory recitative. In both, too, there is the obviously intended acceleration at the change of tempo from 2/4 to 6/8, setting off Don Giovanni's "Andiam, andiam mio bene". This acceleration is forbidden by most conductors today on the grounds that it is not indicated in the score. Mozart and his singers, I believe, would have thought such an indication superfluous, even an insult to their taste and intelligence.

Battistini, by the way, makes a cadential excursion to the high F sharp at the close of the recitative, with a lovely diminuendo on the closing "gioello mio". I think Mozart would have liked it, but doubt that he would have applauded the less tastefully interpolated F sharp at the close of Titta Ruffo's recording of the Serenade. A similarly brash and delightful interpolation is the final leap to a high B flat in Amelita Galli-Curci's 1917 recording of Cherubino's "Non so più". She sings, too, the indispensable appoggiaturas on the repeated "chi m'oda" at the adagio close. Conchita Supervia, on her otherwise charming recording, does not, and the performance suffers accordingly.

To end as we began, with Susanna awaiting her lover in the garden (or pretending to), I have assembled a tape of that aria with and without the recitative, as recorded by Elisabeth Schumann (1923 and 1926), Elisabeth Rethberg (1926), Lotte Lehmann (1933), Audrey Mildmay (1934), Esther Rethy (1937), Bidu Sayão (1950), Elisabeth Schwarzkopf (1952), Irmgard Seefried (1953–54) and Rita Streich (1953).

Schumann's earlier recording is in German, and includes both recitative and aria. Rethberg sings only the aria, in Italian, Lehmann also only the aria, but in German. All four recordings introduce every appoggiatura right where it belongs (in the aria on "bella", "face", "l'auro" and "adesca"). Thereafter, we have a curious and utterly nonsensical uniformity – or non-uniformity. Every artist introduces some appoggiaturas in the recitative, but none sings them all, and no two make the same decisions. None sings any appoggiaturas in the aria.

That brings us to a curiosity. Conductors who, a decade or so ago, would have permitted no appoggiaturas at all, may now *permit,* but not *require,* appoggiaturas in a recitative, leaving the decision up to the singer, as suggested in the recordings just cited. They discourage or forbid their introduction in the arias. This approach, or policy, is reflected in Bärenreiter's *Neue Mozartausgabe,* where appoggiaturas are *suggested* by a symbol over the pertinent note in the recitatives, not always consistently, but never in the arias. This suggests to me a strategic retreat, giving away a little, but not all.

The omission of appoggiaturas in the arias is nonsense. The weak, unmusical cadence on two identical notes is even more distressing in an aria. The singer, in a recitative, can approximate or suggest or imply the missing appoggiatura by conspicuous vocal weight and expressive emphasis on the *wrong* note without actually intoning the appoggiatura. This is more difficult, and may even be offensive in an aria.

Composers of the baroque era and into the early 19th century applied the code to arias just as they did to recitatives, and for the same reasons. Yet today we hear Leonores in *Fidelio*, for example, permitting themselves the unwritten appoggiatura on the first of two identical Es at the concluding "Gatten*lie*be" of her great aria, but omitting it where the same situation arises twice previously on the way to the peroration, and where it is just as obviously obligatory – not to mention the now routinely omitted appoggiaturas on "*Grim*me," "*Stim*me," "Farben*bogen*" and "Meeres*wogen*" in the recitative.

It is mad, maddening, unmusical, inartistic, unauthentic, arbitrary – and even foolish. The introduction of the appoggiatura in one place and its omission in another inevitably throws a spotlight on the sin of omission – and all because of a misreading not of the notes, but of the message the written notes were demonstrably (as we have seen) intended to convey.

What we have experienced over most of this century is conductors and singers reading coded messages without reference to, or in ignorance of, the code; in other words, blithely taking coded messages at face value. Conductors and singers of the generation of Mahler, Lilli Lehmann and Gadski were probably unaware of a key in the form of Telemann's Foreword. They simply observed the conventions passed on from one generation to another from the composer's own time, when the code was so generally and widely understood that its application was taken for granted.

Conductors, coaches and singers of this century, including the most eminent, had good reasons for wishing to curb the undoubted (and abundantly recorded) indiscretions of some star singers, but in proscribing the appoggiatura they have been, as Mackerras suggests, throwing the baby out with the bath water, and strewing the musical landscape, in the opera house, in concert and on record, with thousands of stylistic solecisms – and wrong notes!

Mozart – and not only Mozart – deserves better of conductors, singers, coaches – and critics (where have they been all this time?)!

6

Of Pitch and Transposition

WHAT is *authentic*? What is *original*? And what of the singer? Well, *authentic* and *original* are adjectives much used nowadays by those commendably bent on bringing us operas of the standard repertoire as conceived and written by their authors – at least as far as the music is concerned! – cleansed of the cuts, transpositions, embellishments, cadenzas, interpolations, instrumental touching up, etc., that have come down to us in performance over the years, and are now generally accepted as "traditional", often having found their way into printed vocal and orchestral scores.

Recent examples of this quest of authenticity have been Jesús López-Cobos's edition of Donizetti's *Lucia di Lammermoor* and Alberto Zedda's "authentic" *Il barbiere di Siviglia*. Some seasons ago we had at Covent Garden a *Les Contes d'Hoffmann* laying no claims to authenticity (with this opera there is no such thing), but with the conductor, Georges Prêtre, insisting that everything be sung in the original key as given in the Choudens edition.

Original key – ay, for the singer, there's the rub! Not just *what* was it? More to the point for the singer, *where* was it in terms of the pitch prevailing at the time and place of composition? Our editors, Zedda and López-Cobos, for example, go back to the autographs and find that, let us say, Lucia's final aria, "Spargi d'amaro pianto", is in F rather than the "traditional" E flat, or that Don Basilio's "La calunnia" is in D rather than in C in which it is usually sung.

Well, there those keys are, those tonalities, in black on white in the composer's autograph. Why are not these and other arias now sung in the keys the composers chose for them? López-Cobos has ascribed the downward transposition as far as Lucias are concerned – and the Mad Scene is not the only one – to prima donna vainglory and convenience.

"In order to cope with the top notes asked for by Donizetti," he wrote for a recording of his edition, "they have transposed everything down, making those extra notes and all the extra flourishes easier. . . . I consider it a musical crime to change or even destroy the tonal plan of a great masterpiece for the sake of being able to sing with greater ease a handful of notes (which are not even in the original)."

Plausible enough, if we are thinking only of Lucia. But what of Edgardo and Enrico, who are not prima donnas, and who do not, as a rule, favour or exasperate us with "traditional" altitudinous interpolations, embellishments and cadenzas? As to the keys assigned to *their* music in the autograph our editor is less persuasive. Of the Lucia-Enrico duet, a whole tone lower in the "traditional" version than in the autograph, he wrote: "Incidentally, the high *tessitura* of the baritone in the duet when sung in the original key, like his opening cavatina ('Cruda funesta smania'), reveals a more lyrical character than is customary, one that is in keeping with the youth and impetuousness of Enrico Ashton."

All well and good as interpretive elucidation, but it overlooks, or ignores, the fact that in Donizetti's time there was no such thing as today's high Italian baritone, for whom Enrico's music in the original keys poses no problems. The first Enrico was Domenico Cosselli, described in contemporary accounts as "basso cantante" or "the most celebrated bass in Italy," and who numbered among his roles that of Assur in Rossini's *Semiramide*, now always assigned to those we think of as basses rather than baritones.

Tenors, in the century and a half separating us from Donizetti's Naples of 1835, have edged higher, but not that much higher. And so the original key of D for Edgardo's taxing final scene caused plenty of trouble for José Carreras at the Royal Opera premiere of the López-Cobos edition in 1981. I do not know what passed between tenor and conductor thereafter, but I do know that in a subsequent performance broadcast on Radio 3 he sang it – and to conspicuously better effect – in D flat, as many other tenors have done.

The problem, I venture to suggest, is not one of key, but of pitch. The pitch prevailing in southern Italy was considerably lower than elsewhere. Alexander John Ellis, in his *The History of Musical Pitch* (1880), quotes Carlo Gervasoni's *La scuola della musica* (1800): "The pitch is not the same in all Italian cities. The pitch in Rome is, in fact, much lower than that of Lombardy." The Lombardian pitch at that time, according to Ellis, was A = 422 (oscillations per second, or ops). This was the so-called "classical" pitch common (with variations) in orchestral music throughout Europe until raised later in the 19th century to accommodate the requirements and predilections of wind players. It is about a semi-tone lower than the A = 440 (or a shade higher) that is standard today.

According to Ellis's estimates, the Roman pitch ranged from A = 403.9 down to A = 395.2, which would place it another semi-tone below the "classical" Lombardian pitch, and a full note below our own. Thus, Figaro's high Gs in "Largo al factotum" were F sharps by contemporary standards elsewhere, and Fs when measured against our own A = 440. Don Basilio's F sharps in "La calunnia" were, in fact, the Es that are sung by basses in the transposition from the key of D to the key of C still common today.

It is easy, in retrospect, to see what Rossini must have had in mind. For *Il barbiere di Siviglia* he needed brilliance and sparkle. Had he written for his basses with the conventional *notational* range, their singing would have been low and dull. Here, therefore, he chose higher keys, knowing that what *looked* high to his singers would not, in fact, be as high as it looked.

It seems pertinent to add here that those Gs in "Largo al factotum" should be followed by As on "presto!" They complete the obvious sequential pattern fulfilled in the orchestra. In the autograph, the singer is given a cadence on two identical As an octave lower, Rossini here following the convention adopted by earlier composers of giving singers an option in their shaping of such cadences, but never imagining that the (actually unmusical) cadence would be sung as written.

Thus López-Cobos, in imposing original keys on today's singers, is asking them to sing a semi-tone to a whole tone higher than was required of Gilbert-Louis Duprez, Fanny Persiani and Domenico Cosselli in Naples in 1835. Those downward transpositions of which he complains became "traditional" simply because when *Lucia* went north of the Apennines and the Alps, and was performed at the higher pitches prevailing there, the singers found the music too damned high.

The same had happened with *Il barbiere di Siviglia* twenty years earlier when it journeyed north from Rome. Rosina's contralto music was found congenial by sopranos. Almaviva's music caused fewer problems because Manuel Garcia, Sr., who created the role, was so low-voiced a tenor that he could and did sing Don Giovanni. The trouble lay with the basses (and in Rossini's autograph Figaro, Dr Bartolo and Don Basilio are all listed simply as *bassi*).

Dr Bartolo's "Un dottor della mia sorte" in E flat was too high, and Pietro Romani's "Manca un folia" was substituted. Don Basilio's "La calunnia" was omitted or transposed down to C. "Largo al factotum" was transposed down a whole tone to B flat. Antonio Tamburini even made news of a kind by singing it in B. There it stayed, in performance at least, until the new category of Verdian high baritone emerged to restore it to its original key and make of Figaro a baritone rather than a bass.

From the foregoing it may be seen that transposition for the convenience and vocal health of singers was accepted with far fewer reservations in the previous century than is the case today – or even with none. But singers then had a greater say in the making of artistic and technical decisions than is accorded them now. Consider, for example, this letter, dated 15 March, 1859, from Pauline Viardot to Luigi Arditi, who was to be her conductor in performances of Verdi's *Macbeth* in Dublin:

"Caro Maestro: Here are the transpositions which I am making in the part of Lady Macbeth. The most difficult of all, which will necessitate certain changes in the instrumentation, will be that of the cavatina. The recitative in D flat, the andante, 'Vieni t'affretta', in B flat and the allegro, 'Or tutti sorgete', in D flat, consequently, the whole scene must be a minor third lower. Not bad! All the rest of the act may be given as written. The cabaletta, 'Trionfai', is not sung," etc. – along with composed insertions or alterations to achieve suitable modulations from one key to another.

One can imagine the reaction of almost any conductor today upon the receipt of such a communication. But Arditi cherished it, and was delighted to reproduce it in his memoirs as a letter "illustrative of her clear knowledge of notation and composition as well as her lucidity in dealing in a practical way with the parts which she required to be transposed."

Nor do we have to go back so far to find an example of a great conductor's comprehension and indulgence of a great singer's vocal limitations. In Erich Leinsdorf's profoundly thoughtful book, *The Composer's Advocate* (1981), we find the following about no less puritanical and dictatorial a conductor than Arturo Toscanini:

"Toscanini was also more liberal and pragmatic with transpositions in opera than anyone else in my experience. It has not been recorded that in *Fidelio* performances at the Salzburg Festival he invented a new modulation. The great Lotte Lehmann was incomparably moving and well cast as Leonore/Fidelio, but she had difficulties with the high notes of the aria. When the second run in 1936 came along, Toscanini wanted to relieve Lehmann's anxieties, and transposed the entire piece one semitone lower. Everybody felt that although this was a most generous act to bring out the best in a great artist, the recitative preceding the adagio portion of the aria had suffered in the transposition. . . . In the third year, Toscanini tried to combine the original key of the recitative with a transposed aria, and 'invented' a new transition . . . arriving at the semitone lower key of E flat."

Nor was Toscanini alone in not wishing to sacrifice a great performance on the altar of a semitone. The late Rosa Ponselle told Harold C. Schonberg, then senior music critic of the *New York Times*:

"I had a complex about the high C in 'O patria mia' [in *Aida*] and then [Tullio] Serafin said: 'Why worry? We can transpose the ending a semitone down. Everybody does it. Caruso used to transpose his high Cs down.'" Ponselle added: "I felt pounds lighter!"

In an obituary notice on Mary Garden the same Harold C. Schonberg noted of her recordings of "Depuis le jour" from Charpentier's *Louise*: "Her most famous recording of the aria was made in 1926, toward the end of her career. She had the aria transposed down from G to F, and thus the climax is a high A instead of B. But how easily and beautifully she takes that note, and how elegant is the musical conception, and how purely the voice is projected."

That transposition should have been so common throughout most of the 19th century was essentially the result of wide fluctuations and variations of pitch. As noted earlier, during the 17th and 18th centuries, as far as orchestras were concerned, and thus including opera, pitch had been reasonably stable at $A = 420$, give or take an oscillation or two, in other words, about a semi-tone below today's $A = 440$. Thus, for truly "authentic" performances of just about everything from Handel through Gluck and Cherubini to Beethoven, Schubert, Weber and Rossini, orchestras would have to be tuned down a semi-tone (as is being ever more frequently done now in solo instrumental and chamber music, but is out of the question – because of the construction of the instruments, not to mention the predilections of their players – for modern symphony orchestras), and that Beethoven, exposed to his "Eroica" as played today, would be hearing it in E instead of E flat.

But dating from the time when Tsar Alexander, at the Congress of Vienna in 1815, made a present of higher pitched instruments to an Austrian regiment, of which he was honorary colonel, and whose members were also subject to service in the court theaters, the pitch began to rise, largely because instrumentalists, the winds especially, preferred the greater brilliancy. Instruments had to be adapted to the higher pitches. They could be, and were – including the string instruments. But voices could not be assisted by similar physical and mechanical alteration and adjustment.

The singers' only recourse was to adapt their vocal production to the higher pitch (not an easy undertaking, and least of all with the pitch varying from place to place and from year to year) or transposition to lower keys. There were instances of successful rebellion, most notably by Adelina Patti, Christine Nilsson and the tenor, Sims Reeves, in England, where in some orchestras in the 1860s and 1870s the pitch had risen to a level sensibly higher than today's $A = 440$. Of more enduring effect for England was the insistence by Dr George Cathcart, an ear and throat specialist, that the pitch of the orchestra be lowered to the so-called French diapason ($A = 435$) as a condition for his financial support of Sir Henry Wood in the founding of the Proms in 1895.

But while $A = 435$ and today's $A = 440$ are an improvement on the extremes of the past, there has never been any question of a return to the "classical" pitch of the 17th and 18th centuries. Thus we still have Konstanzes, Fiordiligis, Leonores, Queens of the Night, Florestans and Agathes singing their fearsome arias and concerted numbers a semitone higher than was required of the singers for whom they were written, and who brought less weight of voice to their singing against the less numerous and less clamorous orchestras of their time. As any singer will tell you, a semi-tone can spell the difference between vocal pleasure and vocal distress or disaster.

An example is afforded by the case of the American Minnie Hauk, whose London debut as Amina in *La sonnambula* at Covent Garden in 1868 was a disaster and her second performance a triumph, prompting Henry Chorley to write in the *Athenaeum*: "The chief cause of her greater success was unquestionably the judicious lowering of her principal airs. On the first night she fairly broke down in the final rondo; on the second, when it was transposed a half a note lower, this outpouring of recovered joy became the most thrilling feature of her performance." Chorley went on to attack the abnormally high pitch, probably $A = 450$, or even higher, at Covent Garden at that time.

The case against transposition in opera is that it violates the character and colour associated with the key of the composer's choice (there is, curiously and significantly, no similar objection to transposition in the literature of solo song, with most songs published in three keys for high, medium and low voice), and that, unless applied uniformly to all voices, it violates the composer's structural plan in the sequences of keys from number to number and from scene to scene.

All this is valid, especially for those endowed with absolute pitch (the ability, usually native, to identify any note sounded at random and, consequently, any key). I would suggest, however, that the argument carries less weight today than it would have done a century or a century and a half ago, if only because the adventurous harmonic procedures (and progressions) to which we have grown accustomed in the music of Wagner and his successors have rendered most of us less sensitive than our ancestors to modulations and key changes.

There is, in any case, a certain ambivalence in the opera world as to transposition, especially in respect of tenors, who are frequently allowed downward transposition of Rodolfo's aria in *La Bohème* (to accommodate an alternative high C), the "Di quella pira" in *Il trovatore* (to accommodate unwritten high Cs), the "Salut demeure" in *Faust* (to ease a full-voiced high C for which head voice is more appropriate), and, as we have noted previously, the final scene of *Lucia*. Even the closing duet of Act I of *La Bohème* is sometimes lowered to assist the tenor to an unwritten (and unwanted) final high C, as reflected in the correct answer to the jocular question: What opera act begins in C and ends in B?

Baritones are less often moved to transposition, presumably because, now singing in a range of two octaves from A to A (roughly that of a tenor in the first decades of the 19th century and earlier before continuing upward in head voice and falsetto), they are a relatively new breed, more given to frailty at the lower than at the upper extremes of the range. One transposition generally accorded them, however, is that of Dappertutto's "Diamond" aria in *Les Contes d'Hoffmann* down a whole tone from the E of the printed score to D. This is partly because the role is often assigned to a bass-baritone, rather than a baritone, and partly because two cruelly exposed G sharps in the key of E are no laughing matter even for a high baritone. Yet in the Prêtre production at Covent Garden Siegmund Nimsgern was required to sing it as printed, which he did, making a near thing of those G sharps. And this despite the fact that the aria was drawn from an Offenbach operetta, and only inserted in the Giulietta act by Hans Gregor in Berlin in 1905!

In the end, it is a question of vocal performance and vocal health against a violation of a composer's choice of keys, and I, for one, have no hesitation in choosing in favour of the singer, especially in music dating from a time when the orchestral pitch was a semitone or more lower than it is today. There have been times when, hearing a Donna Anna struggling with "Non mi dir" or a Konstanze struggling with "Martern aller Arten" and "Ach, ich liebte", or a Queen of the Night contending with "Der Hölle Rache", I have thought of founding an SPCS (Society for the Prevention of Cruelty to Singers)!

7

Too Early – or Too Late?

COMPETITION victory, or victories, a promising and well publicized debut, glowing notices, the covers of magazines, then the emergence of a beat (wobble) in the voice, less glowing notices, cancellations, rapid decline and then fade-out, or burn-out – it is a career synopsis all too familiar to opera-goers the world over in recent decades, especially among female singers.

The explanation or rationalization most frequently heard from voice teachers, conductors, coaches and critics is impatience. Young singers start too early, take on heavy roles too soon, often roles ill suited to their native endowment. It was the explanation offered by Sir Colin Davis, then music director of the Royal Opera, at a press conference a few years ago, and it was promptly echoed by the late Harold Rosenthal, then editor of *Opera* magazine, Brian Dickie, general administrator at Glyndebourne, Sir John Pritchard, then musical director of the opera houses in Cologne and Brussels, and vocal pedagogue Vera Rosza.

There are other factors, of course, among them the jet airplane and the proliferation of summer festivals, the first adding jet lag to the physical hazards of operatic demands upon a singer's vocal apparatus, the second robbing the international star of the two- or three-month summer vacations, or leisurely travel by rail and sea, enjoyed by singers in the ages before man began to fly, not to mention a settled family and home life.

But pushing themselves, or allowing themselves to be pushed into big roles and burning themselves out?

That is, I know, received opinion, and has been throughout the sixty-odd years that I have been associated with singers and singing as a student, observer of the operatic scene and personal friend. But historical fact, not opinion, suggests otherwise. Or, to put it more specifically, historical fact suggests that phenomena have occurred over the past two centuries of operatic evolution quite beyond the control of individual singer or singing teacher.

How does one explain, for example, or even comprehend, that at the first performance of Beethoven's Ninth Symphony and fragments of his *Missa*

66

Solemnis on 7 May 1824, the female soloists were Henriette Sontag, aged 18, and Caroline Unger, aged 20? Sontag, less than a year earlier, at 17, had created the demanding role of Euryanthe in Carl Maria von Weber's opera at Vienna's Kärntnerthortheater. She had, in fact, made her opera debut as the Princess in Boieldieu's *Jean de Paris* in Prague at 15.

Then we have Wilhelmine Schröder-Devrient putting Beethoven's *Fidelio* on the map, so to speak, in Vienna in 1822, just one month short of her eighteenth birthday. (Anna Milder-Hauptmann, when she created the role in 1805, was 20.) Schröder-Devrient had made her debut in Vienna as Pamina in *Die Zauberflöte* at 16, and had sung Agathe in Weber's *Der Freischütz* at 17. She went on to be Wagner's first Adriano in *Rienzi*, his first Senta in *Der fliegende Holländer* and his first Venus in *Tannhäuser*.

And so to Maria Malibran, Manuel Garcia Sr.'s elder daughter, one of the legends of opera and vocal history, dead at 28! She had made her debut as Rosina in *Il barbiere di Siviglia* in London in 1825 at 17, and three weeks later partnered Giovanni-Battista Velluti, last of the opera castrati, in Meyerbeer's *Il crociato in Egitto*. Her younger sister, Pauline Viardot, sang Rossini's Desdemona, Rosina and Cinderella at 17 and 18 and went on to create the role of Fidès in Meyerbeer's *Le Prophète*, to sing some 150 performances of Gluck's *Orphée et Eurydice* in an edition especially prepared for her by Berlioz, and to give the first performance of Brahms's Alto Rhapsody. She lived to within two months of 89!

We move on, then, to Giulia Grisi, making her debut in Bologna at 17 and, in 1831, singing Adalgisa to Giuditta Pasta's Norma in the premiere of Bellini's masterpiece at 20 (Pasta was then a ripe 34, with sixteen years of opera singing behind her). Grisi continued on to a long and glorious career in an enormous and wide-ranging repertoire in Paris, London, St Petersburg and New York, especially remembered as the soprano of the so-called "*Puritani* Quartet" (with Rubini, Tamburini and Lablache) and as the first Norina in Donizetti's *Don Pasquale*.

Nine years younger than Grisi was Jenny Lind, who, in Stockholm in 1838, made her debut as Agathe in *Der Freischütz* at 17. This was modest compared with Adelina Patti, who toured in concert from the age of 7, made her operatic debut as Lucia at 16 (in New York in 1859) and was an international star at 18. She was still singing (and recording) in her 60s.

As we move on through the 19th century, we find Lilli Lehmann singing Pamina at 17, Ernestine Schumann-Heink making a debut as Azucena (!) in

Dresden at 17, and Pauline Lucca as Elvira in Verdi's *Ernani* at Olmütz at 18. It would be possible to name many more who were singing major roles in their teens. Those who made their debuts in major roles in their early 20s are too numerous to list. Suffice it to say that they were the rule rather than the exception, and that most of them continued on to enjoy long and glorious careers. Schumann-Heink took her leave of the stage as the Erda of *Siegfried* at the Met on 11 March 1932, three months short of her 71st birthday.

In our own century we have had Conchita Supervia singing the first Roman Octavian at 15, Rosa Ponselle appearing for the first time on any opera stage with Caruso as Leonora in *La forza del destino* at 21, Kirsten Flagstad making a debut as Nuri in D'Albert's *Tiefland* (a secondary but exacting role) at 18, and, most recently, Maria Callas singing Tosca (!) in Athens at 17 and adding Santuzza, Marta (*Tiefland*), Leonore (*Fidelio*), Gioconda, Aida, Turandot, Isolde, Kundry, Brünnhilde and Elvira (*I Puritani*) to her repertoire while still in her teens and early and mid-20s.

A random selection of twenty of the foremost female singers born in the half-century between 1860 and 1910 yields an average age of 20 for a debut in a leading role in a reputable house. One would expect the average age for male singers to be higher, if only because the process of mutation has to be completed before the category and quality of a voice, not to speak of musicality and inclination, can be determined. It *is* higher, but only slightly. A similar random selection of thirty of the foremost male singers born in the same period yields an average debut age of 21. The list *does* include some males who made their debuts at 18 or 19.

The most spectacular career in terms of age among the males, and one that offers, I think, a clue to what has happened in the past century, is that of Julius Schnorr von Carolsfeld, who created the role of Tristan in Munich in 1865 at 29, just a month short of his thirtieth birthday, and died six weeks later in Dresden after singing, as Don Ottavio, a rehearsal of *Don Giovanni*. It is that Ottavio that provides the clue.

A Don Ottavio singing Tristan cannot have sounded like Lauritz Melchior – or any other Tristan whom any of us can remember. Schnorr, who had been engaged at Karlsruhe at 18, and was a principal tenor there at 22, also sang Tannhäuser and Lohengrin, and was preparing Siegfried when he died. What it means, I suggest, is that in the intervening century *our vocal expectations have changed*. Today, in those big roles, we expect more voice.

The suggestion is reinforced by what we can still hear of the older singers on record, and what we know of the variety of roles they sang. Lilli Lehmann, for example, sang the Brünnhildes and Isolde, and even Ortrud and Fricka, but she also sang Lucia, Konstanze, Rosina, Gilda, Violetta and even Carmen. As we can hear from her records, made in 1905 and 1907 when she was pushing 60, she could not, as Brünnhilde or Isolde, have sounded like Flagstad and Birgit Nilsson.

As we listen to their records today, we find it inconceivable that a Patti could have sung Aida, that an Eames could have sung both Aida and Santuzza, that a Margarete Siems could have been both the first Marschallin and the first Zerbinetta, or that Irene Abendroth, whom we hear singing so fluently the "Bel raggio lusinghier" from *Semiramide* in a recording made in 1902, could have been the first German Tosca and a memorable Sieglinde.

The big voices that emerged from the latter half of the 19th century and the early decades of the 20th – Ruffo, Caruso, Gadski, Austral, Leider, Flagstad, Muzio, Ponselle, Turner and many more – all set examples and standards that encouraged, even required, emulation – and ruined many voices. Singers have been tempted, or urged, to take too much chest voice too high, to push their voices rather than float and sustain them. Even today's coloraturas no longer have the girlish sound treasured in a Sontag, a Grisi or a Lind, and still audible – and treasurable – on the records of Tetrazzini, Galli-Curci, Hempel, Siems, Ivogün, Eames and even Patti in her early 60s.

Our ears have become accustomed to a bigger, more mature, ampler, fuller sound, and to the association of a particular sound with a particular role. An Erda can no longer sing Lucrezia Borgia and Fidès as Schumann-Heink did, or both Ophelia in Ambroise Thomas's *Hamlet* and Carmen and Santuzza as Calvé did, not to speak of combining Tristan with Don Ottavio. Only Callas, in our time, has covered so wide a territory, and it may well be that in striving to accommodate contemporary expectation in the heavier roles she incurred vocal damage that subsequently blemished her singing and shortened her career.

Some will argue – and do – that the older singers had the advantage of smaller houses. Some houses were, indeed, smaller, but it is pertinent to note that Milan's La Scala dates from 1778, Naples's San Carlo from 1817, Turin's Teatro Regio from 1738, Philadelphia's Academy of Music from 1857, Vienna's Staatsoper from 1869, the Paris Opéra from 1875 and New York's (old) Metropolitan Opera House from 1883.

What grew bigger – and louder– was the orchestra. It is well to remember that the earliest of the singers named here did not have to contend with the size, importance and sound of the orchestra as it evolved and expanded under Verdi, Meyerbeer, Wagner and Strauss, and that the oldest of them did not have to contend with an A = 440 pitch. Moreover, their listeners had neither heard nor dreamt of such music, nor, of course, had they heard Ruffo, Caruso, Melchior, Flagstad and Nilsson.

The result in recent years has been that young singers, less richly endowed and technically inferior, resort to "pushing" in an attempt to emulate those to whom the big sound was either native or acquired by technical mastery. What we hear is a "breathy" vocal production, the breath escaping ahead of the voice, or with the voice, that may sound imposingly in a small room or a small house, but which spreads and is dissipated in a larger auditorium against a large orchestra.

Older singers with smaller voices overcame the handicap by a concentration of tone, getting 100 per cent in vocal return for every ounce of breath expended. It was thus that an Elisabeth Schumann, for example, could always be heard in the largest houses. Today's youngsters are wasting breath and energy, and in taking too much voice too high they end up yelling instead of singing. What I have found most disturbing in recent years, both in the professional area and in the schools, is that what I hear as yelling is being found acceptable by younger teachers and critics.

What also has changed, it would seem, is the pace of maturation, especially among females. Education, too, has probably had something to do with the retarded pace of professional development. Many of the older singers were born into theater or musical families, and literally grew up in the theater. They could launch a career without thought of the insurance of a university degree. Their education and sole preoccupation, aside from the three Rs, was musical, vocal and dramatic. Today's singers in their teens and early twenties have much else on their minds and in their curriculum, most prominently the prospect of a secured future as a tenured teacher in the event of professional failure or decline – or at least failure to achieve professional stardom – as can be expected in at least 90 per cent of the individual cases. And so, having invested eight precious years in securing at least an MA, they embark on a professional career not too early, but too late.

To return to the factor of impatience with which we began, it does play a part, not so much among those who have arrived – although it undoubtedly plays a part among them, too – but among the beginners in their late teens and early, sometimes late, twenties. As guest lecturer at the Summer Vocal

Institute of the Dallas-based American Institute of Musical Studies in Graz, Austria, I have listened to some 1,500 auditions in nearly twenty years, and to many auditions elsewhere. The pattern is always the same – singers tackling arias they are far from equipped to handle. Why do their teachers permit it? One reason is that the arias are required for qualification and categorization. A second, as I have heard from the teachers, is that if the student is discouraged from taking them on, the teacher is accused of being "non-supportive", and the student changes teachers.

But granting a young singer an exceptional endowment, sound schooling and a promising debut, the real villain of the piece is probably the jet airplane, and not just because of the ill effects of jet lag or the physical effect of sudden changes of climate, weather and environment. When I look at the itineraries of top singers in the pages of *Opera* and *Opera News*, I find myself asking: Is that any way to live?

There are still houses, primarily in German-speaking central Europe, but also now in Great Britain, where a singer can lead a resident and artistically rewarding professional life. But to achieve international recognition – and the big fees and recording contracts! – he or she must crash the international jet set, and, having crashed it, face competition of the fiercest sort and, of course – the jet!

8

The Lowdown on High Notes

DOES your heart beat for Manrico at that moment in the third act of *Il trovatore* when the militant rum-da-da-dum-dum in C major announces "Di quella pira"? Of course it does. You wonder whether he will make those two high Cs – and so does he!

But if Manrico, whoever he may be, is in a bit of a spot, he has only himself and generations of previous Manricos to thank for it. And you in the audience, too. Verdi did not put him there. According to oral tradition, Enrico Tamberlik (1820–89) did. Julian Budden, in Volume 2 of his three-volume *The Operas of Verdi* (1978), drawing on a public lecture by Giovanni Martinelli, tells the story thus:

"Before asking his [Verdi's] permission to include the note in question, Tamberlik had already experimented with it in various provincial theatres where, he told the composer, it was in great demand with the public. 'Far be it from me,' Verdi had answered, 'to deny the public what it wants. Put in the high C if you like, provided it's a good one.'"

Those high Cs in "Di quella pira" are the most famous and the most striking examples of the difficulties singers have made for themselves by offering more than the composer requires. They are not unique. The baritone's high A flat in the *Pagliacci* Prologue is an interpolation, as is the final G. Neither is appropriate to the text, however appropriate it may be to the melodic line. The same is true of Rodolfo's unwritten and abominable high C at the close of the first act duet of *La Bohème*, although this may be passed up without the tenor's disgracing himself. Most of the soprano high E flats and Es at the end of their big scenes are interpolations, including such traditionally obligatory examples as those that round off "Caro nome" and "Sempre libera", not to mention all the wild things that have been done, and are still done, with "Una voce poca fa", originally written for a contralto, and extending upwards only to a high B (a high A at Rossini's Roman pitch of 1816).

The tradition of *ad libitum* high notes is about all that is left of the singer's privilege, clearly understood by composer and performers alike in the 18th and

19th centuries, of embellishment and melodic deviation. Even cadenzas, nowadays, are commonly stereotypes, handed down from generation to generation and often considerably abbreviated. This tradition is a curious anomaly at a time when, in every other area of Serious musical activity, the composer's written notes are accepted as holy scripture, and their violation condemned as sacrilegious.

The same critics who would howl at an unindicated ritard in the "New World" Symphony or at the slighting of double-dotted notes in an 18th-century French overture, take for granted the substitution of an A flat and a B double flat for the notes Verdi deemed appropriate to Rigoletto's final "maledizione!" – not to mention the A flat without which no baritone would dare to end the "Si, vendetta!" They even accept – if they notice – the downward transposition of "De quella pira" and "La donna è mobile" by tenors not sure of their Cs and Bs. The rationalization is that neither pedantry nor reason nor taste nor discretion nor respect for the composer's intention nor regard for the singer's vocal health can dispel or extinguish the thrill of a free, ringing, exultant, defiant high note.

In male singers, of course, such notes are associated in the audience's mind with virility. It is in this sense that one speaks of vocal matadors. Many a tenor has seen in the contours of the letter C the canted symbol of a bull's horns. His life is not at stake, but his reputation is; and in Italy, at least, where an opera house may quickly assume certain of the characteristics of an arena, his failure can be greeted by demonstrations hardly less disgraceful than those accorded a matador who has made a cowardly kill – or none at all.

The suggestion of sexual prowess would seem to be less obvious on the female side, but the risk is there, and all the excitement and tension associated with the hazardous. The rewards of success and the penalties of failure are the same as with males. In either sex the blooming top is the symbol and the glory of a singer's vocal maturity, and its fading is commonly the first evidence of decline.

The appeal of the vocal high note is not, in any case, essentially musical. The highest note of a phrase is normally the climactic point in the melodic arch, whether the phrase is sung or played. But no one would argue that high notes at the extremes of the violin or piano have the same effect as the tenor's high C or the soprano's high E flat or E, or the baritone's high A flat. There is little of the element of derring-do. The high note of the trumpet comes closer to it, and with the trumpet we have again the evidence of physical power and prowess.

Indeed, the analogy between trumpet and voice is documented in the account of Farinelli's triumph over a trumpet player – outdistancing him, so to speak, in compass and length of breath – in Rome early in the 1720s at the beginning of the career of that most celebrated of the *castrati*.

High notes were not so essential to the *castrati* as they subsequently became to the unmutilated males who succeeded them in opera's heroic roles at the beginning of the 19th century. The best of them had the high notes, particularly in their youth, and they made good use of them; but the music written for the *castrati* seldom ascends above the high C, and very little of it goes as high as that. Many of the *castrati* who began as sopranos, moreover, retreated to the mezzo-soprano range early in their careers without loss of status, and some of the best of them were mezzo-sopranos to begin with, notably Bernacchi, Senesino, Carestini, Guadagni (Gluck's first Orpheus) and Pacchierotti.

Nor were the greatest female singers of the age of *bel canto* celebrated for their high notes, although some had them. The greatest singers of that time, male and female, may have had such an abundance of more musical virtues that they could disdain the athletic triumph of the high note. But high notes exerted a fascination then as now, and they added lustre to the careers of certain singers, mostly female, reminiscent of the high note glory of such singers in our own century as Erna Sack and Miliza Korjus.

The most famous of those early high note singers was Lucrezia Agujari (1743–83), more familiarly and less elegantly known as La Bastardina, or La Bastardella. Mozart heard her in Parma in 1770, and wrote down one of her cadenzas that had taken her to the C *in altissimo* – that is, an octave above the soprano's normal high C.

According to the musical historian Charles Burney, however, Agujari achieved these altitudes by employing falsetto, in other words, a kind of fourth-dimensional head voice probably similar to that used by Emma Calvé in some of her recordings, or to the detached kind of head voice demonstrated in more recent years by Lily Pons. Burney preferred Anna Lucia de Amicis (*c.* 1733–1816) who, he said, was "the first singer I had ever heard go up to E flat *in altissimo* with true, clear and powerful *real* voice." Since Burney goes on to say that Agujari "ascended much higher, but in falsetto", it is clear that his *in altissimo* refers to the E flat above the soprano's normal high C.

Since one does not usually associate falsetto with female voices, it seems pertinent to note here that it has been widely employed in our own time by popular female singers, especially by blacks. I have heard Cleo Laine and Ella Fitzgerald sing up to Agujari's high C *in altissimo* in falsetto, and both are, by native vocal endowment, contraltos. Instead of making the opera contralto or mezzo-soprano's passage (*passaggio*) at about D or E flat, they and others simply go through it into falsetto. Burney gives Agujari's normal range as the two octaves from A to A, suggesting that she, too, may have been a contralto, or at least a mezzo-soprano.

It is significant that this specific attention to high notes becomes conspicuous in vocal history only in the second half of the 18th century – in other words, when the age of *bel canto* began to exhibit signs of decadence. There can hardly be any doubt that the high note phenomenon was a symptom of decline. When merely beautiful singing no longer sufficed, the astonishing high note was a last resort, an unwitting acknowledgment of desperation.

The same can hardly be said of the subsequent importance of high notes to unmutilated males. They were more fitting to the new high tension genre of opera, especially the operas of Meyerbeer and Verdi. Tenors and basses enjoyed only a secondary status in the age of *bel canto*, when the sound of the male voice, and particularly the bass, was felt to be a bit vulgar, and better suited to *buffo* roles. When the heroic roles came their way with the disappearance of the *castrati*, they – the tenors, at least – were not immediately prepared to provide the truly masculine sound required by the new taste for romantic melodrama.

Many of the tenors and basses of the age of *bel canto* had been schooled by *castrati*, and they were guided and judged by the same criteria, especially the tenors, emphasizing the languishing *cantilena*, appropriately embellished, and the *aria d'agilità*, calling for brilliancy of execution rather than booming high notes. If they took to higher altitudes – and they sang, indeed, higher than any tenor sings today – they did so in a light head voice or falsetto, the sound at the upper extremes of the range resembling the male alto or counter-tenor of today.

We can hear echoes of this kind of tenor vocalism on the records of some of this century's finest singers, notably Fernando de Lucia, Tito Schipa, Miguel Fleta, Giacomo Lauri-Volpi, Richard Tauber, John McCormack and Richard Crooks, but they have rarely used it exclusively, even in any one aria. Lauri-Volpi, for example, in his recordings of "A te, o cara" from Bellini's *I Puritani*, uses it superbly, but spoils the enchantment by a stylistically anachronistic full-voiced high C (transposed down from the unwritten D flat of the original).

He and his fellows, no doubt, dared not do otherwise for fear of being thought of as effeminate or vocally inadequate.

There was a singular and sudden abundance of excellent tenors in Italy in the first decades of the 19th century, an astonishing number of them coming from Bergamo and its environs. Some of them, notably Giovanni David (or Davide) (1789–1851), had high-pitched voices with a considerable extension in falsetto. David used to interpolate cadenzas taking him as high as the F above high C. Parts written for him by Rossini – the role of Roderigo in *Otello*, for example – took him to the high D as a matter of routine. But the way the notes occur, almost always in *fioritura*, is evidence, if any were needed, that David did not sing them in chest voice. The same is true of the music written for the even more famous Giovanni-Battista Rubini (1795–1854).

None of their contemporaries ever claimed for these tenors a note higher than a B in full voice, and the astonishment excited in the 1820s by Domenico Donzelli (1790–1873), who sang an A from the chest, suggests that David and Rubini, when they ascended much above an F or a G, did so with a *voix mixte* (a mixture of chest and head resonance) rather than the full chest tones of subsequent tenors. The high Cs of the last act of *William Tell*, for instance, which later brought such fame to Gilbert-Louis Duprez (1806–96), had so little effect as sung by Adolphe Nourrit (1802–39), the first Arnold, that until Duprez came along the act was omitted in Paris, and the opera languished.

It is with Duprez and these high Cs that modern tenor high-note history begins, specifically on 17 April 1837, when Duprez made his debut as Arnold at the Paris Opéra. There is a curiously moving account of that occasion in Berlioz's *Evenings in the Orchestra*, curious because neither Duprez nor the opera is identified, although the details correspond precisely to the circumstances of Duprez's debut:

"A number comes during which the daring artist, *accenting each syllable*, gives out some high chest notes with a resonance, an expression of heart-rending grief and a beauty of tone that so far no one had been led to expect. Silence reigns in the stupefied house, people hold their breath, amazement and admiration are blended in an almost similar sentiment: fear. In fact, there is some reason for fear until that extraordinary phrase comes to its end; but when it has done so, triumphantly, the wild enthusiasm may be guessed. . . . Then from 2,000 panting chests break forth cheers such as an artist hears only twice or thrice in his lifetime, cheers that repay him sufficiently for his long and arduous labors."

One hopes that they also repaid Duprez's subsequent premature loss of his voice. He had discovered his full-voiced high C during the Italian premiere of *William Tell* in Lucca in 1831 (he was later, in 1835, to create the role of Edgardo in Donizetti's *Lucia*). Until then he had been just another lyric tenor, and rather small-voiced at that. When he first sang at the Odéon in Paris in 1825 it was said that one had to be seated in the prompter's box to hear him. He was selected for the role of Arnold at Lucca only as an emergency replacement for the mezzo-soprano Benedetta Pisaroni. He knew that the kind of voice he had employed heretofore would be inadequate for the big scenes of *William Tell*, and in his own words, as recorded in his *Souvenir d'un Chanteur* (1880), "it required the concentration of every resource of will power and physical strength. So be it, I said to myself, it may be the end of me, but somehow I'll do it. And so I found the high C which was later to bring me so much success in Paris."

Rossini could not complain, as he often did of other singers, that Duprez had presumed to improve upon the composer. There is not just one written high C in the *scena* under discussion, but seven. Berlioz's account, with its "expression of heart-rending grief", would seem to refer to a single high C in a cadenza at the close of Arnold's aria, "Asile heréditaire", where he sings "Je viens vous voir pour la dernière fois", the C falling on the *nier* of "dernière". But the following *cabaletta*, beginning with "Amis, secondez ma vengeance", has six exposed and sometimes sustained high Cs, plus an unwritten one at the close, now usually sung– when the scene is sung at all – à la "Di quella pira", of which the whole *scena* is an obvious prototype.

Rossini first heard Duprez's high C in his (Rossini's) own home several years later, and expressed his opinion by looking to see if any of his precious Venetian glass had been shattered. It struck his Italian ear, he observed, "like the squawk of a capon being garroted". And he foresaw, correctly, that Duprez's success would inspire emulation and even more hazardous exploits.

The prophecy was fulfilled when Tamberlik interpolated a high C sharp in the last act of *Otello*. Rossini was furious. When Tamberlik came to pay his respects to him in Paris, Rossini is said to have sent word that the tenor would be welcome, but that he should leave his C sharp in the vestibule and retrieve it as he left. The score of *William Tell*, incidentally, includes a C sharp that Duprez did *not* sing. "That tone", Rossini used to say, "rarely falls agreeably upon the ear. Nourrit sang it in a head voice, and that's how it should be sung."

Despite Tamberlik's C sharp – and many other tenors have subsequently accomplished it – the high C natural has remained the tenor's proper ceiling. Something happens to the sound, if not the voice, when this ceiling is extended, even with the most superbly endowed tenors. The voice loses body and amplitude. My own preferred ceiling is a B flat, or at most a B.

It is similar with the baritone A flat, although an A natural, given the right voice, is more acceptable than the tenor C sharp or D flat. Many baritones have had a B flat, and some have had a high C. But above the A natural as the upward limit, the voice takes on a tenor-like quality. It tends to thin out, and the optimum effect is lost. Tenors and baritones alike, when they venture beyond these apparently natural ceilings, risk diminishing returns as well as vocal damage.

The escalation, so to speak, of the lower male voices is less easy to pursue and document. There is no single dramatic incident such as Duprez's high C in *William Tell* to signal the entry into a new era. Indeed, it is impossible even to fix the time when baritones came to be separated from basses, unless it be with Verdi's *Ernani* (1843), in which the baritone role of Carlo, when the opera was first given in London in 1847, was found by Giorgio Ronconi (1810–90) and Antonio Tamburini (1800–70) to be so high that they refused to sing it, leaving it to the mezzo-soprano Marietta Alboni (1826–94).

In the age of *bel canto* there had been just tenors and basses, the latter singing normally within the two-octave span from F to F at the lower pitch of the time. Confined to secondary roles in *opera seria*, they had found more congenial employment in *opera buffa*, and the most famous of them, Luigi Lablache (1794–1858) and Tamburini, made their initial fame as *buffo* basses before Rossini, Donizetti and Bellini gave them roles in which they could prove themselves equally accomplished as serious singers and actors.

The singer with whom the modern baritone category begins was probably Francesco Graziani (1829–1901), whose voice was described by the English music critic Henry Chorley as "one of the most perfect baritones ever bestowed upon mortal." He is the first bass or baritone of whom one reads (in the 1954 *Grove*) that "his voice, though not extensive downwards, had beautiful and luscious tones, reaching as high as G and even A." One wonders where he put that A! In an earlier generation he would probably have been classified as a tenor. But when Graziani came along, the tenor top (in full voice) had already moved up a minor third from A to C.

Thirty years separated Graziani from Lablache and Tamburini, and in the interval there had been Ronconi, for whom Verdi wrote *Nabucco* and Donizetti

Torquato Tasso, and Filippo Coletti (1811–94), who, although not the first Germont, was the first great one. A third historically important baritone was Felice Varesi (1813–89), the first Rigoletto, the first Macbeth and the first Germont.

Nothing that one reads of these three singers, however, suggests a prototype of today's high baritone. They were referred to variously as baritones, basses and *bassi cantanti*, and were equally famous in *buffo* roles. Ronconi and Varesi, particularly, had serious vocal deficiencies. Indeed, Chorley credited Ronconi with barely an octave. It is unlikely that any of them added gratuitous high notes.

But the roles written for them provided the opportunity for Graziani and Antonio Cotogni (1831–1918) to establish a new intermediate category, and to separate forever the baritones from the basses. The reference to Graziani's G and A suggests that he may have been the first to add to the baritone range the extra notes that composers subsequently came to take for granted. Varesi as Rigoletto, for example, if he sang only what Verdi had written, would not have had to sing above a G flat except for one passing and usually unnoticed G in the Quartet.

If mezzo-sopranos have been less inclined, as a rule, than other vocal categories to interpolate high notes, it is probably because they have troubles enough with what is already given them. No singer in her right mind, certainly, would wish to improve on the difficulties contained in the role of Fidès in Meyerbeer's *Le Prophète*, written for Pauline Viardot (1821–1910). Besides, the mezzo-soprano who can easily sing higher is more likely to take over soprano roles (as Viardot did) and aim for the higher fees as well as the higher notes.

During the formative years of grand opera in the first decades of the 19th century, the contralto, like the bass, was constrained to sing secondary or supporting roles. With the disappearance of the *castrati* she was so frequently assigned male parts that the designation *musico*, formerly applied euphemistically to the *castrati*, was passed on to contraltos specializing in them. Arsace in *Semiramide*, Tancred in *Tancredi* and Maffio Orsini in *Lucrezia Borgia* are examples of what was expected of them.

These are not conspicuously high parts, and that of Arsace, especially, indicates a kind of singer whose glory was at the bottom rather than the top (a kind of feminine baritonal glory that today's mezzo-sopranos are either unable to duplicate or, if able, reluctant to exhibit, and often subject to pedagogical and critical disapproval if they do). Nor, with the exception of Tancred, which was quickly appropriated by sopranos, were they starring roles. There was always a soprano above them. As with the basses of that time, contraltos, as stars, were reckoned better suited to *opera buffa*. Rossini, in *Il barbiere di Siviglia*, *La Cenerentola* and *L'Italiana in Algeri*, gave them some of their most congenial roles, and extended their upper range. The ability to scale vocal heights, and the opportunity to do so seem to be essential to operatic stardom.

But *opera buffa* was not enough for such ambitious women as Giuditta Pasta (1798–1865), Maria Malibran (1808–36) and Viardot, her younger sister. These were mezzo-sopranos without a dramatic mezzo-soprano repertoire commensurate with their talents as singing actresses, and they simply extended their upper ranges by assiduous study and practice, moved in on their soprano sisters and took over – not, it should be added, without vocal consequences similar to those that befell Maria Callas as the price of heeding ambition rather than discretion in her choice of roles.

Not until Meyerbeer conceived the role of Fidès for Viardot in 1849 was there a proper role for a mezzo-soprano (Adalgisa in *Norma*, now usually sung by a mezzo-soprano, was written for Giulia Grisi (1811–69), a soprano, and that of Leonore in *La Favorite* for Cornélie Falcon (1814–97), a dramatic soprano, and first sung by Rosine Stoltz (1815–1903), whose voice is variously described as a soprano or "high mezzo"). Verdi followed with Azucena, Eboli and Amneris, Gounod with Sapho, Saint-Saens with Delilah and Bizet with Carmen. Wagner added enough to the repertoire to keep mezzo-sopranos busy for the rest of foreseeable time, and most of these parts are high enough to discourage any improvisatory upward extension.

The problem for sopranos, being at the top to begin with, and accorded the privileges and fees pertaining thereto, has been a question not of altitude, but of weight, amplitude and volume. No soprano has sung higher than Agujari, nor have there been any arias of more distressing *tessitura* than those of the Queen of the Night. But it was one thing to sing high in the light, girlish tones favored in the age of *bel canto*, and perpetuated in the vocalism of such later singers as Patti, Melba, Tetrazzini and Galli-Curci, and quite another to bring to a high C or D flat the forcefulness of utterance required of Verdi's and Wagner's soprano heroines.

The high C required of an Isolde, an Aida or a Turandot is equivalent to the tenor's high C from the chest. It requires bringing the middle voice, or a good deal of it, up beyond the natural passage to the head register, normally at an F or F sharp. And it cannot be done habitually without loss of lightness, ease and flexibility at the upward extreme of the vocal compass. But while tenors simply abandoned the extreme upper notes (above high C) and the *fioriture* common to their kind in the age of *bel canto*, sopranos split up into the now familiar categories of "dramatic," "lyric" and "coloratura". To each her own, and to each her own high notes.

To the latter, including her mezzo sisters, also goes, unfortunately, the privilege of altering a composer's design for her own vocal convenience. I am not speaking of ornamentation or other occasional and often effective melodic deviation, but of the now universally accepted and adopted convention of laying out (as a jazzman would put it) for a few measures in order to catch a deep breath before attacking an ultimate or penultimate high note, thus wilfully destroying the momentum established by the composer to give his singer a brilliant close. A survey of pertinent recordings suggests that this abominable practice began to creep in about 1920, and it has been with us ever since. Its acceptance by conductors and critics at the very time when more and more was being made of conscientious observation of the composer's script is one of the many paradoxes of 20th-century vocal history.

If singers have tended, as a rule, to move upward because *up* is where the glory and the money are, there are certain high-note problems that cannot be charged to their own ambition, vanity and greed. These have been imposed by composers, and in almost every instance they have been a cause of embarrassment and exasperation rather than vocal satisfaction. Left to their own devices, singers will interpolate a high note where it can be attacked most securely and where it will do the most good – the A flat in the *Pagliacci* prologue, for example. Composers, to whom a high note can never mean what it does to a singer, tend to put them where they are most difficult to reach, least effective when arrived at, or both.

There are various ways in which wily Iagos and Beckmessers can fudge over the high As as for Iago's Drinking Song and Beckmesser's Act III, Scene 3 exit. But this is not true of the murderous high A required of the Captain of the Pinafore in his tender address to the moon. The exposed high C in "Salut, demeure" in Gounod's *Faust* was almost certainly never intended to be sung in full voice, but nowadays few tenors can sing it any other way, and even fewer would dare to try it if they could. The *macho* syndrome again. Isolde's high Cs are real and inescapable – and likely to be drowned in the orchestral flood. There is no way of escaping the pianissimo high D flat at the close of the sleep walking scene in *Macbeth*, although one way around it has been found in hiring another soprano to sing (off stage) just that one note. Equally inescapable is Aida's fiendishly exposed high C in "O patria mia". No possibility of an off-stage substitute there! Only the impossible (for most tenors) pianissimo B flat at the close of "Celeste Aida" has been turned to the singer's advantage. The tenor simply belts it out.

Whether imposed by the singer upon himself – and, if successful, upon others, who cannot then be inferior – or by the composer upon the singer, the high note and the high *tessitura* have become ineradicably institutionalized. One may complain that they have nothing essentially to do with music, that they represent athletic or acrobatic rather than melodic or lyrical achievement, that they inhibit the singer's ability and will to apply himself to worthier objectives, and that they shorten vocal life. It is all to no avail. And many of us would be more or less secretly sorry if it were not so.

9

Opera as Propaganda

WRITERS of programme notes, opera guides and liner notes have feasted for years on the benighted contributions of Italian and other European censors to the ultimate shaping of opera librettos. Verdi, Donizetti and others, and their librettists, were frequent victims. The transformation of Victor Hugo's *Le Roi s'amuse* into *Rigoletto* is a famous – or infamous – example.

Twentieth-century enlightenment has sweetened the commentators' pot with revivals restoring the librettos to their original time and locale – not always with enlightened consistency. I remember, for instance, a revival of *Il ballo in maschera* at the Met, during the Edward Johnson regime, which returned the story from Boston to the Sweden of Gustave III, but still had the choristers hailing "il re d'Inghilterra" with pre-revolutionary zeal.

It is easy to tax the censors with undue and pedantic severity, and to laugh at the fractured history often born of desperate compromise. But it is just as easy to forget that crowns sat uneasily on European heads following the French Revolution and the Napoleonic wars, and that opera had become a popular rather than a primarily aristocratic diversion. Tales of rebellion were favourite fare, and it is hardly surprising that governments found them tediously unwholesome.

Although we may have forgotten – if we ever knew – that one opera did, in fact, set off a rebellion, the censors certainly did not. That was Auber's *Masaniello*, more familiarly known as *La Muette de Portici*, the story of a Neapolitan rebellion led, significantly, by a humble fisherman in 1647. A performance of *Masaniello* in Brussels on August 25, 1830, sparked a rebellion against Dutch rule, and led to the establishment of an independent Belgium.

Auber probably did not intend to start a revolution with *Masaniello*, nor Rossini with *William Tell*. Verdi's intentions with *Nabucco*, *Ernani*, *I Lombardi*, *La battaglia di Legnano* and *Un ballo in maschera* may have been less innocent. But in any case the subject matter then in vogue in a period alive with the new pulse of democracy was always potentially inflammatory.

The pitiable pleasures discovered by Beethoven's prisoners in *Fidelio* in a few moments of sunlight and fresh air may not have been expressed in musical accents sufficiently catchy for the European middle classes or proletariat. And in *Fidelio* the political dose is diluted by giving Pizarro a benevolent superior and a reluctant, if venal, warden. But the homesickness of the Jewish prisoners of Babylon in *Nabucco* and the marches in *Masaniello* were couched in strains that none could escape and that all could both feel and sing.

In fairness to the censors, it should be noted that their strictures were based on tradition as well as political immediacy. Not many years had passed since opera composers, as court employees, had lent themselves as a matter of course to the propagation of the royal faith. They were especially useful in providing royal births, weddings and coronations with appropriate allegorical tributes to the virtues, real, imaginary or hoped for — of the illustrious personages concerned. Metastasio's *La clemenza di Tito* was considered especially suitable, and not even Mozart seems to have had any political qualms about setting it for the coronation of Leopold II as King of Bohemia.

For 200 years, operatic emotions had been too often constrained to unadventurous sentiments. The chorus, the real villain of the piece in 19th-century opera, had played a secondary role, if any. The principal characters were of divine or royal blood, and endings were satisfactorily happy. To the censors of the 1830s and 1840s the predilection of composers and their librettists for virtuous bandits, dissident commoners and restless peoples was as novel as it certainly was exasperating.

But if composers, with the possible exception of Verdi, have rarely worked for a specifically revolutionary objective, or been witting propagandists beyond the choice of a subject matter attractive to a large audience in a time when revolution was fashionable, the fervour of their music, and the accident, perhaps, of an appropriate story, have often been exploited by others.

Mozart could not have foreseen that the Soviet Army would reopen the Staatsoper in Vienna in April, 1945, with *Le nozze di Figaro*, casting an approving eye on the proletarian assertions implicit in Figaro's deportment. Nor could Beethoven have imagined the propagandistic complexities of the reopening of the Theater an der Wien in the following October with *Fidelio*, when the Russians had to applaud a production ostensibly celebrating the liberation of Austria from Nazi tyranny, fully knowing that the Viennese were far more deeply concerned with the hope of liberation from their Soviet liberators.

Least of all could Christoph Willibald Gluck have imagined *Alceste* being used by Nazi propagandists in Dresden in 1933, its heroine's sacrifice employed as a symbol for an obscure agitator named Schlageter, shot by the French during the post-World War I occupation of the Ruhr. (Schlageter's role as an Alcestian martyr was short-lived. There were too many who insisted that he had really been a communist.) And, speaking of communists, Bizet would probably have been more amused than outraged at communist productions of *Carmen* in eastern Europe designed to show that headstrong and ill-disciplined female as a proletarian heroine.

But not all propaganda is political. Once we eliminate politics, two operas come immediately to mind, loaded with propaganda. One is *Die Meistersinger*. The other is *Feuersnot*. Wagner was always a propagandist – but in his early operas the message is nothing more portentous or controversial than the nobility of the self-effacing, self-sacrificing female. This is an underlying theme, too, of *Der Ring des Nibelungen*, although diluted by the audience's – and Wotan's – sympathy for Brünnhilde's initial disobedience, by Siegfried's dubious heroism and the sordid and selfish villainy of just about everyone else. It recurs in *Parsifal* and *Tristan und Isolde*, although the ambivalence of the respective females is too complex for effective propaganda.

Die Meistersinger is quite another matter. If we are accustomed to think of it as the least problematical of Wagner's music-dramas, it is because analytical attention is so often centered on the benign figure of Hans Sachs. The character of Beckmesser is, of course an attack on anti-Wagner critics, specifically Eduard Hanslick, and as such is obviously a propagandistic device. Far more subtle and therefore more effective propaganda is concealed within the inoffensive figure of Walther.

We tend to think of him as a conventional romantic hero, forgetting, or overlooking, the singular and significant circumstances of his defeats and victories. It is not the winning of the contest for Eva's hand that counts in Wagner's plan, but rather the fact that victory is achieved in spite of, or even because of, Walther's ignorance of and indifference to the rules of the game. Translating the contest of song into the contest of life, we see the artist – namely Wagner – claiming for himself a privileged position in society in return for the blessings issuing from his divine calling, entitled by his divinity to ignore or violate the conventions and inhibitions imposed by society upon its mortal members – as Wagner did with respect to other men's money and other men's wives.

While not everyone may agree with this interpretation of Walther, there can be no reasonable doubt about the implications of Kunrad, the hero of *Feuersnot*. The opera was conceived as a rebuke to the city of Munich for its failure to perceive the virtues of Strauss's first opera, *Guntram*, in 1894. The story is of a young artist caught in an elopement and chastised with philistine severity. The artist, who is capable of magical as well as poetical wonders, deprives the city of fire, in other words, warmth and light. Needless to add, the good burghers quickly acknowledge the error of their philistine ways, and permit the blessed unity of beauty and genius. To render his message blindingly clear, Strauss makes his hero the pupil of an older master, Reichart by name, who had previously suffered under the benighted Münchner.

Neither *Feuersnot* nor *Guntram* has since been popular in Munich or anywhere else. But we still have "Ein Heldenleben" to remind us of the high opinion certain German composers held of themselves in those days, and which contributed so much to popular acceptance of the composer's claim to autonomy in deciding what is good and proper fare for ordinary mortals. We do not usually think of all this as propaganda, but then, just as the greatest art is that which disguises art, so is that propaganda the most effective which is so artfully accomplished that it is not recognized or thought of as such.

Lack of subtlety has been the prevailing weakness of most contemporary operatic propaganda such as Gian-Carlo Menotti's *The Consul*, Luigi Dallapiccola's *Il prigioniero* and the Weill-Brecht *The Rise and Fall of the City of Mahagonny*. Menotti's opera, while hardly revolutionary, is certainly a witting rebuke to the inability, incapacity or unwillingness of bureaucracy to cut red tape and accommodate the requirements of fugitive revolutionaries, victims, presumably, of oppressive tyranny. It is moving in its sincerity and compassion, but weakened by the naive assumption that consular inhibitions, determined and regulated by international law and agreement, could be dissolved by a sudden burst of universal goodness.

More specifically, it overlooks the fact that, while the consul could issue the fugitive's wife a visa, he could not issue the exit permit without which the visa would be useless. That could come only from the ministry of the interior of the (unnamed) country involved. The opera's credibility is further damaged by the reckless return of the fugitive and the improbable violation by the secret police of consular extraterritoriality, not to mention the melodramatic and gratuitous device of having the unseen and unidentified consul exposed as a crony of the police agent.

Il prigioniero lacks even the relief of Menotti's scenes with the magician, and in *Mahagonny* the obscenity of the human race is laboured with tedious single- and simple-mindedness.

The day of opera as a medium of propaganda is probably over. It was never an effective medium for political argument, or any other kind of argument, as demonstrated in Strauss's *Capriccio*, if only because music is an art of emotional rather than ideological or ideational communication. In the days when new operas had wide popular appeal, in the 1830s and 1840s, when stirring music was fashionable, and its listeners easily stirred, it was an effective propaganda auxiliary, whether composers were conscious propagandists or not. Many of the operas of that period are still popular and still stirring, but the excitement they generate is unrelated to contemporary political or esthetic issues.

Insofar as contemporary operas concern themselves with ideas, political or otherwise, they favour either a discursive style, as in *Capriccio*, with its lengthy dialogues about the respective priorities of words and music – much of the text, and therefore much of the argument, inevitably lost in the orchestral "commentary" – or the grim, brutal pessimism of Dallapiccola, the relentless insistence and intensity of *verismo* without the infectious persuasion of Mascagni's and Giordano's soaring melodies. The contemporary composer seems to forget his communicative purpose, or at least the requirement of a common and compelling musical language.

Auber, Spontini, Donizetti, Verdi, Rossini and even Wagner, whether witting propagandists or not, addressed their audiences in a musical language mutually felt and mutually understood. This was what made the censors uneasy. Most contemporary composers, excepting Menotti – and he has paid a price for it with the critics – do not. The language of the librettists may be intelligible English, German, French or Italian, however awful most of it usually is, simply as prose or poetry. But the music escapes the lay listener's heart, which the composer can reach ahead of the orator or pamphleteer – if only he can humble himself to find and speak a musical language to which it responds.

IO

A Vocabulary of Vocalism

ONE evening, many years ago, a group of us were gathered together in a friend's apartment in New York during one of Dame Eva Turner's visits to the United States, and the talk, inevitably, was of singers and singing. "Madame So-and-So," the legendary Turandot and Aida from Lancashire was saying of a certain soprano known to be in vocal trouble, "carries her chest too high."

Everyone in the group was professionally concerned with music, although not necessarily with singing, but a look at the faces of her auditors, as Dame Eva made her pronouncement, left me with the sudden realization that probably half of those present assumed that she was referring to Madame So-and-So's embonpoint. If so many in so musically sophisticated a circle, I thought, would not know immediately that Dame Eva was referring to Madame So-and-So's handling of the "passage" or transition from chest register to middle register, what of the poor layman exposed, in reviews and in conversation, to the jargon of vocal comment and criticism? How confusing and bewildering it must be.

Well, some of it can be pretty baffling to the professional, too, even the vocal professional. The terms may be familiar, and the professional who uses them sure enough in his own mind what they mean, but they don't always mean the same thing to all professionals, and in some cases there have been century-long disputes as to whether they mean anything at all.

About some terms, happily, there is general agreement. In the classification of voices, for example, bass, tenor, contralto (or alto) and soprano are standard categories, now commonly extended to admit bass-baritone between bass and tenor, mezzo-soprano between contralto and soprano, and coloratura soprano above soprano. Normal two-octave ranges for these categories would be E to E for the bass, F to F for the bass-baritone, G to G for the baritone, B flat to B flat for the tenor, F to F for the contralto, A flat to A flat for the mezzo-soprano, B flat to B flat for the soprano and D to D for the coloratura. These are, of course, mean ranges, subject to extension in both directions and varying from voice to voice.

Until about the middle of the last century there were no marked differences of type or range within the basic categories. A soprano, for example, was a soprano. It was expected of her, however, that she be able to meet a variety of requirements, and this expectation was taken into account by the composer in laying out the sequence of her principal scenes. An *aria cantabile* would show what she could do with a languishing *cantilena* (sustained song), with emphasis on a fluent *legato* (the seamless binding of one note to another). A more forceful number, possibly an *aria di vendetta*, or vengeance aria, would give her a chance to pull out all the vocal and emotional stops. An *aria di bravura*, or *aria di agilità*, would show off her range and agility in a kind of virtuoso display now described as *coloratura* and including trills, *staccati* (detached notes), roulades (also referred to as runs or divisions) and so on.

Each of these arias would normally be introduced by a *recitativo* (recitative) passage in which the dramatic setting or pretext for the aria would be established, and in which the singer would demonstrate her command of declamation. This variety was often combined in a single scene, or *scena*, arranged in the sequence: *recitativo, aria, cabaletta*, the latter giving the singer a brilliant, virtuosic close. A familiar example of this sequence, much favoured by Verdi, is provided at the close of Act I of *La traviata* where Violetta has the three episodes beginning respectively with "è strano", "Ah, fors'è lui" and "Sempre libera".

Singers of other categories were similarly provided for, according to their abilities and specialities. With the growing size of the theaters and orchestras in the first half of the 19th century, however, and with the increased weight of voice required for the dramatic and heroic outbursts of Meyerbeerian, Verdian and Wagnerian opera, not to speak of Strauss, Mascagni, Puccini and Giordano, singers found it impossible to be all things to all composers and all operas. The limit of versatility, for sopranos, at least, was probably reached by Verdi with Leonora in *Il trovatore* and Violetta in *La traviata*.

Singers might conceivably be able to sing both Brünnhilde and Norma, both Carmen and Konstanze. Lilli Lehmann did, and there have been others. But, generally speaking, excellence in one department was achieved or enjoyed at the expense of facility in another. Not many singers can shift easily from the weight of voice required by Turandot to the airy flexibility expected of Lucia, as Maria Callas, in our own time, did, and even of Callas it can hardly be said that she was equally at ease in both, or that her ambitions did not shorten her vocal life.

And so, where once there had been just sopranos, there are now the dramatic soprano, the lyric soprano and the coloratura soprano. Where formerly there had been just tenors, there are now the Heldentenor (heroic tenor), the dramatic tenor (*tenore di forza* or *tenore robusto*), the lyric tenor (*tenore di grazia*, *tenore leggiero* or the slightly deprecatory diminutive *tenorino*), the *spinto* (a lyric tenor pushed toward the dramatic – Gigli, for example, or Bjoerling, or, closer to our own time, both Domingo and Pavarotti).

With the exception of the coloratura, who was expected to sing higher than other sopranos, there was not much difference in the ranges required of these types. Nor was it simply a matter of the natural size of the voice. It probably had just as much to do with how much voice the singer was inclined or persuaded to produce, especially in the upper fifth of the range. It was a question of how much voice he or she was prepared or accustomed to spend on those top notes that brought off the dramatic climaxes, brought down the house, and brought in the cash.

Which leads us to the question of registers. Here we leave the area of common agreement for an area endlessly contested. The registers are generally assumed to be three: low, middle and high, or chest, middle and head. But some singing teachers have denied that there is any such thing. Even those who believe in registers will agree that the terms are largely metaphorical, or figurative, representing an attempt to illustrate or define processes of vocal production that have not, despite the laryngoscope, ever been identified to the common satisfaction of all concerned.

One thing only is certain. Most singers, of every category, have a physical or muscular problem (easily soluble, initially, for the exceptionally endowed) in extending their range or compass up or down much beyond about an octave and a third. A great deal of the jargon of singing centers on this problem of extension.

An opera singer friend of mine in Vienna, many years ago, put it about as simply and vividly as I have ever heard it put. "Singing", he said, "is just one unending struggle with the Adam's apple." The professional singer solves (or tries to solve) the problem of extension by controlling the larynx, by learning to keep it out of the way, and by adjusting the weight of the vocal tone, or the weight of the breath on the vocal cords, to what the traffic will bear at any given pitch or sequence of pitches. Most singers, when being examined by a throat specialist, will wave off the wooden tongue depressor. They have learned to depress, or they haven't learned to sing.

Whether or not one thinks of registers as metaphorical or actual, there is no doubt that something muscular is accomplished, enabling the singer to move fluently up or down into a region barred to the untutored and the unpracticed. This something is called the passage, also called "register break". Some singers recognize two such passages – one as they move from middle to lower register, the other as they move from middle to upper. For many singers it is the most hazardous spot in the vocal range, neither one thing – or register – or another. Its difficulties can be exploited, too. The knowledgeable listener hears a tenor, for example, showing signs of distress around F or F sharp, and thinks: "My God, he'll never make it to that B flat!" Then comes a glorious B flat, and the effect is the more telling for the previous anxiety and suspense. Martinelli offered many an exciting example of this.

In negotiating the passage and moving beyond it, the singer tries to remain "above" the tone, not in the sense of being above the pitch, but rather in the sense of being above, and in control of, the vocal situation, or avoiding, in other words, being choked by his own vocal apparatus. It is a matter of getting up and over – and of staying there.

The question of "staying there" introduces another much used term: *tessitura*. The Italian word means "texture", but as used in vocal jargon it refers to the area of the singer's vocal range where a song or an aria or an opera lies *most of the time*. It is often more important and more problematic than mere location of the lowest and the highest notes. Many a tenor, for example, is less terrified of a piece containing a single high C than of a piece with nothing above a B flat, but with lots of Gs, G sharps and As. Edgardo's *ultima scena* in *Lucia* is a serviceable example.

There is muscular exertion in singing beyond the normal octave-and-a-third range, whether the listener is aware of it or not, and, ideally, he should not be. It is not a question of forcing the tone, although that may also play a role, but rather of subduing rebellious or recalcitrant elements in the muscular apparatus. If this exertion has to be sustained, the controlling faculties are likely to tire, and the singer is in trouble.

The technical devices employed to overcome these physical problems are many, varied, and sometimes controversial. The terminology employed to identify and describe them is imprecise and mystifying. There are also the kinds of voice one employs in these registers: chest voice, full voice, head voice (*voce di testa*), mixed voice (*voix mixte*), half voice (*mezza voce*) and so forth.

These all relate, basically, to the weight of breath upon the vocal cords. As with the bow upon the strings of a violin, or the breath upon the reeds of an oboe, clarinet or saxophone, the greater the weight of breath, the bigger the tone – and the greater the resistance and exertion. More breath is required the higher one sings. Singers who learn to moderate the weight of tone to accommodate the exertion sing higher – and longer. But they forgo the excitement generated by the big tone at the top of the range. Some singers, equipped with more strength than skill, can ascend only by giving all they have.

There are advantages and disadvantages in each. Mathilde Marchesi, the most celebrated moulder of women's voices in vocal history, herself a pupil of Manuel Garcia, favoured the more moderate approach, and achieved in a score of famous pupils a wonderfully even (or equalized) seamless scale from bottom to top and from top to bottom, insisting on her pupils' easing off as they got over the passage – or into the head, as it is often described – and on their so mastering the passage that it was indiscernible to the listener and, probably, with ultimate control, to the singer, too.

The result, as can be heard on the records of Nellie Melba and Emma Eames, was the epitome of refined vocal virtuosity, and Marchesi's singers were vocally long-lived. But this kind of singing tended to be bland. Composers of the latter half of the 19th century, moreover, were demanding stronger stuff, and there were singers delighted to oblige, whatever the cost. Emma Calvé left Marchesi to become the Carmen and Santuzza of her generation, and Geraldine Farrar, ignoring Melba's advice, rejected Marchesi as a teacher in favour of Lilli Lehmann.

The fashion of forceful utterance required of singers that they carry as much as feasible of the weight and resonance of the normal middle voice into the upper areas. Just how much is up to the singer's skill and discretion. Those who are longer on strength and daring than on skill or discretion, tend to become very loud, and some of them, especially tenors, have become very rich. They also tend to be vocally short-lived. The muscles that depress easily in youth become less amenable with age and wear and tear.

This is what the talk is about when you read or hear of the "high C from the chest", the *ut de poitrine* which entered vocal history and vocal terminology with Gilbert-Louis Duprez's full-voiced high Cs in *William Tell* in Paris in 1837, discussed in greater detail elsewhere in these pages. Again, the term is purely figurative. Prior to Duprez's time, a middle ground had been favoured, a combination of head (again, a figurative term) and chest, called a *voix mixte* or mixed voice, the French terminology being the more common because French tenors were especially good at it. Depending upon the mixture, it considerably extended the singer's upper range, and for those who favoured something closer to a pure head tone, this meant, for tenors, pitches well above the high C.

It would be easy to generate a debate by attempting to define or establish the border between head voice and *mezza voce*, although it may help to remember that *mezza* means "half". Definition becomes even more problematical when trying to distinguish absolutely between head voice and *falsetto*. According to an old rule of thumb, a properly sustained head tone could be returned from pianissimo to full voice without a discernible break, whereas a *falsetto* tone could not. And it is generally agreed that the vocal production employed in yodeling is *falsetto*.

Falsetto brings us, inevitably, to the category of counter-tenor, or *haut-contre*, again a tricky term that has been applied to many types of voice − or vocal production − ranging from the very high operatic tenor to something we think of today as being closer to the adult male alto or soprano. In this latter sense it has almost vanished from the operatic scene. But the vogue of 18th-century opera revivals has found the counter-tenor a possible solution to the casting of parts originally written for *castrati*. Some counter-tenors insist that they are not falsettists. I leave it to the specialists, knowing that they will be untroubled by doubt, but seldom in agreement with one another.

After such problematical phenomena of vocal terminology, it is a relief to turn to one that is not problematical at all, however much misused: *messa di voce*, a term that laymen − and not only laymen − tend to confuse with *mezza voce*. It comes from the Italian *mettere* (to put), and means literally, "the putting of the voice." In the age of *bel canto*, the *messa di voce* was the device of attacking a note pianissimo, swelling it out to the maximum intensity, then diminishing it to the original pianissimo and beyond, all in one breath. It was often used to begin a song or aria, and this probably explains why so many of the songs and arias of the period begin, textually, on the exclamations "O" or "Ah".

Some other common terms are more easily defined. "Attack", for example, refers simply to the way a tone is initiated, or launched. A clean attack is one that begins precisely on pitch, and with the voice properly focused in terms of register, colour and intensity. Attacking by a sudden, slightly violent, closing of the vocal cords, as in a cough, is what is meant by the *coup de glotte*, literally a "blow" on the glottis, the opening between the vocal cords.

If the tone is attacked from below, one speaks of "scooping". Something like the same kind of attack, if employed intentionally as a device of expressive phrasing, is called "slurring". This may occur more commonly in the passage from one pitch to another, acceptable or not depending upon the musical context and the singer's purpose. If unintentional, it is usually deplored as evidence of sloppy vocal habits and as vitiating the normally desired *legato*. If intentional, it may contribute effectively to the articulation of text and phrase.

When such slurring is applied to notes widely separated, it is called *portamento* from the Italian *portare* (to carry). In the past half century this has been discouraged as synonymous with slovenly phrasing or unwarranted liberty by fashion unable to distinguish between slovenliness and virtuosity, but it can still be relished on the records of older singers (Claudia Muzio comes immediately to mind). Domenico Corri, cited previously, in his *The Singer's Preceptor* (1810) called it "the perfection of vocal music" and justly comparable to "the highest degree of refinement in elegant pronunciation in speaking." To hear an illustration of what Corri was talking about, one must turn today not to the opera house, but to Frank Sinatra.

Vibrato and *tremolo* are vexatious terms, used for both instruments and voices, and most frequently when there is felt to be too much of either – or too little. All voices give some sense of vibration, or *vibrato*, deriving from slight but regular unevenness in the passage of breath over the vocal cords. Otherwise, a voice sounds "white", "straight" or 'hooty". The character of the vibrato has a good deal to do with the character of the voice.

Whether a very fast, narrow, conspicuous *vibrato* is found to be irritating or delightful can be a matter of taste – and fashion. What one hears on old records from such singers as the tenors Fernando de Lucia and Alessandro Bonci and the mezzo-soprano Conchita Supervia would not be heard with relish by many singers today, nor be approved by many pedagogues and critics. For younger listeners it takes some getting used to, but patience may be well rewarded.

A very slow or wide *vibrato* can also be irritating, and here patience and accommodation may be less well rewarded. I remember old Italian opera connoisseurs in my native Philadelphia describing a very wide *vibrato* as a *permanente*, or permanent wave. They were probably referring to an uncontrolled irregularity proceeding from faulty production or vocal wear and tear, more commonly termed nowadays a "beat". A controlled wide vibrato can be attractive. It is not often heard these days in the opera house. Here, again, we have to look to the popular singers, particularly Sarah Vaughan.

Another example is Billy Eckstine, who once described his objective in the employment of *vibrato* to me thus: "I think of it as like dropping a pebble into the smooth surface of a pond, and watching the ripples spread out from the point of entry." The effect, when listening to a Vaughan or an Eckstine, can be magical.

We come, finally, to "placement". Among singers and singing teachers the talk is endlessly of "placing" the voice, of "focus", which means about the same thing, of "forward" production, of "singing into the mask", of "throaty" production, and so on. Again, one is dealing with figurative terms. There is no such thing, really, as "placing" a voice. The tone originates in the larynx, and passes through resonating cavities in the head. Talk of placement or of production has to do largely, I suspect, with things happening – or not happening – with the larynx, the soft palate, the pharynx, etc., which enhance, inhibit, restrict or modify this normal process. There is no such thing, certainly, as a "mask". But when the inhibiting factors are dormant, or under control, there is a sense of forward, nasal resonance.

In reviewing all this, it occurs to me that I have dealt more with subjects than with definitions. And that, I fear, is about all one can do. It is what makes the study and discussion of singers and singing so fascinating. One can learn what has to be done and, in a general way, how it should be done. But there are many ways of describing both, all more or less inexact. And beyond the imprecision lies the simple fact that no two singers, in their physical endowment, are precisely alike.

"That", said Joan Sutherland in an interview for *Life* Magazine some years ago, "is why there aren't many good singing teachers. We have the sensations inside us. They only know what they hear outside. You ask two singers how they get a particular note, and they'll describe exactly opposite feelings – and what they're doing may be exactly the same thing. Actually, singers are the last people anybody should ask about voice production."

Marilyn Horne, in the same interview, summed it up when she said: "What happens is that over a long period of time and practice you find the sensations that work and then put a name to it that means something to you."

II

Tracking Down the First and Oldest Recorded Singing Voice

WHO is the oldest singer in terms of year of birth to have been recorded? The question was put to me over lunch in Stockholm in March of 1974 by Gunnar Ahlén, music critic of *Svenske Dagbladet*. I replied, as most collectors would have done: "Antonio Cotogni, an Italian baritone born in 1831." A more accurate reply, as I have since learned, would have been: "Jean-Baptiste Faure, a French baritone born in 1830." He recorded "Viens Lénore" from Donizetti's *La favorita* on a Pathé cylinder in Paris, probably about 1900.

"No," said Ahlén, "I have a recording by a Danish bass named Schram, a pupil of Manuel Garcia, who was born in 1819." Was I interested? I was.

I gave a lecture that evening under the auspices of the American Embassy. Ahlén covered for his paper. He came up to me afterwards, pressed a tiny spool of tape into my hand, and said: "Here he is!"

Back home in London, I put the spool on my tape recorder and, to my astonishment, heard an obviously elderly gentleman singing Leporello's entrance aria from *Don Giovanni* and a fragment of his "Catalogue" aria, unaccompanied (except for characteristic cylindrical background noise and some clicks) and in Danish. What to do about it?

The first thing, obviously, was to confirm the existence of a Danish bass named Schram who could have been born as early as 1819. No such name is to be found in any standard – or not so standard – history of opera or singing, or in any lexicon in English, French, German or Italian. But as I am the fortunate possessor of a replica edition of the fifty volumes of the Leipzig *Allgemeine Musikalische Zeitung* from 1798 to 1848, with a supplementary volume of index, I turned to the latter and found: 'Schramm [sic], baritonist in Copenhagen, Vol 49 (1847), p 199." There, in a "Letter from Copenhagen", I read:

"The baritone department at the Royal Theatre is splendidly represented by Herr Hansen and Herr Schramm. . . . Both are endowed with beautiful, rich voices, and both have been well schooled. Herr Schramm, unfortunately, must content himself with deep bass roles, as we do not have a true deep bass, and this will, in time, have a damaging effect on the natural beauty of his voice."

In 1847, Schram, if born in 1819, would have been 28. So far so good, but not far enough. When, and under what circumstances, was the recording made, and from what did Ahlén make the tape he had given me? I wrote several letters to him requesting further information, but received no reply. In the meantime I played the tape for a number of knowledgeable friends. All tended to the view that the recording was a fake. I was unable to subscribe to this opinion. If anyone were going to fake something of this kind, I reasoned, he would not have chosen a singer unknown outside Denmark singing Leporello in Danish.

I turned in due course to the Danish Embassy in London. A biographical lexicon in their library had a substantial entry under "Schram, Peter, born September 5, 1819 [and thus just thirteen months older than Jenny Lind], died there July 1, 1895," establishing him as having been one of the most distinguished actors and singers in the long history of the Royal Theatre, his career there covering sixty-three years, forty-seven of them as a singer (1841–89), the rest as an actor, beginning as a child walk-on in 1832.

So much for the existence and identity of Peter Schram. But what of the recording? Flemming André Larsen, press and cultural attaché at the Danish Embassy, knew of a programme on the Danish Radio called 'I Would Like to Hear," which included a "Discophile Corner". If a cassette transfer of my tape were broadcast on this programme, he suggested, it might elicit the pertinent information. It did.

In preparing the programme, broadcast on 21 September 1978, the producer, Mogens Landsvig, consulted a *Gramophone Book* by Knud de Hegermann-Lindencrone, and learned that the Schram recording had been made in 1889 in the home of Consul-General Gottfried M. Ruben, a coal and coke merchant and early enthusiast of Edison cylinders. Following the transmission, Landsvig was told by another collector and authority that Hegermann-Lindencrone actually owned most or even all of the Ruben cylinders and that, during the 1930s, had transferred a number of them to disc. These discs, said Landsvig's informant, are extremely rare, and he knew of no one who had a copy. (Gunnar Ahlén, obviously, did.).

The key figure, then, in what was now becoming less and less a mystery, was Hegermann-Lindencrone. He was not listed in the Copenhagen telephone directory, but through collector friends I was able to get his address – or addresses, as he divided his time between Denmark and Mallorca – and initiated, in February 1979, a fruitful correspondence. Here is the story of the Ruben cylinders as he told it in reply to my first letter:

"One day in 1936, the director of Polyphon, Dr. Hamburger, phoned me about a man with some cylinders in which Polyphon was not interested. He gave me his name, Consul-General Ruben's son, Victor. I phoned him. He told me about Schram and many others. We made a rendezvous. It was a rather modern house next door to one of Copenhagen's nice bars, Wonderbar, and I told myself, going up to the third floor, that with such an address it would all turn out to be just a misunderstanding.

"Well, there they were, three wooden boxes with those cylinders. He gave them to me and, a few days later, agreed to let me re-record some of them. Polyphon accepted, and we set up a subscription in our paper, the *Berlingske Tidinge* (the world's oldest newspaper, founded in 1749), of which I am a co-owner. One day, a month or so later, in the Odd Fellows studio, on my handmade EMG gramophone connected with one of my phonographs (an Edison), we did it: two 12″ discs, one with singers and one with actors, all very famous Danish names, fifty copies each, plus my test pressings.

"All Ruben's cylinders were safely protected in solid wooden boxes, each with two shelves and each shelf with three ranges of eight cylinders. They were placed each on its own wooden socket with the name and the title pasted on the sockets. Shortly after Victor Ruben's donation to me, three more boxes were recovered from the Danish Polytechnical Institute where they had vegetated for nearly fifty years following the introduction of Edison's improved phonograph (with wax replacing Edison's original tinfoil).

"That was in 1888. It was demonstrated at the Danish Polytechnical Institute in 1889, and it would seem that Ruben, who was already recording profusely, lent those three wooden boxes for the demonstration, keeping the most interesting for himself. The Institute subsequently lost interest, and so it was that only some fifty years later Victor Ruben remembered that the boxes were still there. He phoned the Institute, and arranged that they be turned over to me.

"The greater part of Ruben's cylinders were by Danish artists whose voices have not been recorded elsewhere, several bearing their vocal signature together with a statement of the exact date of recording, ranging from the late 1880s to the late 1890s, some in good condition, others completely smashed. This Schram cylinder, fortunately, was in what collectors call 'mint condition' as to the grooves, only slightly marred by a dozen severe clicks.

"Ruben used to entertain artists from the Royal Theatre and private theatres at his home after performances, and would record them informally in the course of a convivial late evening. The Schram cylinder was thus recorded following a special performance of *Don Giovanni* on 5 September 1889, marking both his 70th birthday and his retirement as a singer. No other performance of *Don Giovanni* was given in that season.

"Shortly before the release of these disc transfers, a test copy with Schram's Leporello was played on 2 April 1937, at a gramophone concert sponsored by Radiolytteren in the Hindsberg Koncertsal. Victor was present, and also the Danish historian, Robert Neiiendam, founder of the Danish Theatre Museum. After the concert, Neiiendam come rushing up to me exclaiming, 'It is exactly as he sang in his later years, and as I remember him!' Neiiendam was born in 1880, and might well have attended that farewell performance as well as his subsequent performances as an actor."

These *Don Giovanni* extracts, although acoustically primitive as recordings, are of more than merely antiquarian interest and significance, notably with regard to style and performance practice. The turns, appoggiaturas and flourishes applied to Mozart by a student of Garcia merit the attention of singers – and conductors, too – in our musically literal age. The same embellishments may be heard, as I have recounted in my discussion of the appoggiatura, on the 1903 recording of "Non più andrai" from *Le nozze di Figaro* by Sir Charles Santley, born in 1834, and also a student of Garcia.

Aside from some appearances in Stockholm, probably with Jenny Lind, who sang with him in Copenhagen in 1843, Schram seems never to have sung outside Denmark with the exception of a single concert in St James's Hall, London, on 21 July 1863, about which *The Musical World* reported in its issue of 8 August: "He sang three times, a French air, two German airs and two Danish romances, all in his native tongue. It was curious to hear the Catalogue Song from *Don Giovanni* in Danish. It was well sung, however, and that is the chief thing required. Herr Schram was encored in Schubert's 'Wanderer' and in one of his Danish romances. . . . The attendance was small and Danish."

Schram cut two other cylinders for Ruben, both of a Danish folk song, "The Carpenter with the Fifteen Children", his encore specialty, and probably the romance referred to above, but both were broken. He subsequently made, according to Hegermann-Lindencrone, two commercial recordings, one of Mephistopheles' Serenade from Gounod's *Faust* and one of Dr. Bartolo's aria from *Le nozze di Figaro*, for A.V. Swendsen, the founder in 1901 of *Dansk Fonograf Magasin*. They could be heard in Swendsen's phonograph shop at Amagertov in the centre of Copenhagen by dropping a coin into one of those legendary slot machines. Neither of these two cylinders has come to light.

Their loss is less to be regretted than that of six cylinders known to have been made in 1890 by the great German baritone, Julius Stockhausen (1826–1906), one of the finest and most influential singers of the 19th century and the first to sing the song cycles of Schubert, Schumann and Brahms in public. He, too, was a student of Garcia in both Paris and London.

In a long letter to the Bern, Switzerland, *Der Bund* (No. 253, 13 September 1890) from Frankfurt, where he taught, Stockhausen praises the Edison machine as a 'phonographic vocal coach'', superior to the echo as a detector of failings, and tells of having himself recorded three cylinders of pedagogical substance and three songs: Schumann's "Frühlingsnacht", Brahms's "Wiegenlied" and the first of Schubert's "Müllerlieder".

He refers to this letter in a letter to Brahms from Thun, in Switzerland, dated 13 September 1890, closing with: "It's a true story, and I would not be surprised if your 'Magelone' were to travel to America on electric wings." It was not to be in Stockhausen's time, of course, with the playing time of a cylinder limited to two minutes. But no trace of the cylinders has been found.

In the unlikely event of the Stockhausen cylinders turning up and proving to be playable, this would not disturb Schram's distinction of being not only the oldest singer in terms of date of birth to be audible on record, but also, to the best of my knowledge, the first opera singer to be recorded. Stockhausen was seven years younger than Schram, and his cylinders were made, presumably, a year later.

The Schram recording is not, as of this writing, commercially available. The Sterling Collection at Yale University has one of the 1936 discs, and I have given cassette copies to the Rodgers and Hammerstein Collection of the New York Public Library, to the British Library Sound Archive and to a number of private collectors.

12

A Centenary the Met Overlooked

HE centenary of New York's Metropolitan Opera House was duly and appropriately celebrated on 22 October 1983. A second centenary should have been observed a year later, on 24 November 1984, but passed without notice. It was that of the seven-year stretch during which the new house was home to what may well have been, for five or even six of those seven years, a finer German (and Austrian) opera ensemble than any in German-speaking central Europe.

It is essential to remember that the Metropolitan Opera Company, as it was then called, was not a company in the sense of an artistic ensemble or theatrical enterprise. It was a real estate company. It did not produce opera. It leased the premises to an impresario who did. During the inaugural 1883/84 season, the house was leased to Henry E. Abbey. The season was an artistic success, but a financial disaster.

The Board, accordingly, was sympathetic to a proposal by Leopold Damrosch (1832–85) that he take over the house for the production of opera by German artists in German. Damrosch had come to New York from Breslau in 1871 as conductor of the Männergesangverein Arion. He had founded the Oratorio Society in 1874 and the Symphony Society in 1878. He could thus provide orchestra and chorus locally, and recruit singers from the German and Austrian opera houses at fees far below what Abbey had paid to Christine Nilsson, Marcella Sembrich and others. He would use sets and costumes bought for Abbey. With a New York German population of something in the order of 250,000, he would have a prosperous and appreciative public. It was a deal.

The accomplishments of that company, or companies, in the first year under Damrosch and thereafter under Anton Seidl (1850–98) make heady reading. In those seven 14–15 week seasons, extending roughly from November to March, the company staged thirty-six operas from the German, French and Italian repertoires, including sixteen first American performances and the first Met performances of *Aida* and *Die Walküre*. Everything was sung in German.

The high point of this Teutonic occupancy was the first American staging of the *Ring* cycle between 4 and 11 March 1889 (although not uncut, and interrupted by a matinée of *La Juive* on 9 March). This had been brought about gradually: *Die Walküre* in the opening season under Damrosch; *Siegfried* and *Götterdämmerung* in the season of 1887/88 and, finally, *Das Rheingold*, given its American premiere on 4 January 1889.

There had been other important American premieres, notably those of *Die Meistersinger* and *Rienzi* in the season of 1885/86 and *Tristan und Isolde* in 1886/87. Outside the Wagner canon there were first American performances of such exotic (and exacting) matters as Goldmark's *Queen of Sheba* and *Merlin*, Weber's *Euryanthe*, Nessler's *Der Trompeter von Säkkingen*, Spontini's *Fernand Cortez* and Ignaz Brüll's *Das goldene Kreuz*.

The company averaged just over sixty-two performances of an average of fifteen operas each season. All this with rosters of solo singers averaging just over thirty-three. (London's Royal Opera, for its 1988/89 season, listed 127 singers for nineteen operas!) In 1886/87 there were only eleven females, and in the seasons of 1887/88 and 1889/90 only twelve. Remarkable enough! But when we come to the conductors, we are face to face with the prodigious.

In the first season, Leopold Damrosch conducted fifty-one performances of twelve operas in 101 days, including the first Met production of *Die Walküre*, averaging just under a performance every two days for two and a half months. Small wonder that he caught pneumonia and died on 15 February 1885, leaving his son Walter (1862–1950; subsequently to become a household name in America as virtually the inventor of "music appreciation" in public appearance and on the radio) and an assistant conductor, John Lund, to finish the season.

During the six years of Seidl's reign there were only two conductors, himself and Walter Damrosch, and Seidl did most of the conducting. In the season of 1887/88, for example, he conducted fifty-five of sixty-five performances, including the American premieres of *Siegfried*, *Götterdämmerung*, *Der Trompeter von Säkkingen*, *Euryanthe* and *Fernand Cortez*. The remaining repertoire for that season embraced *Tristan und Isolde*, *Die Meistersinger*, *Fidelio*, *Tannhäuser*, *Le Prophète*, *Lohengrin*, *La Juive*, *Faust*, and *Die Walküre*. Walter Damrosch conducted *Le Prophète*, *La Juive* and *Faust*.

Such a repertoire and such accomplishments were possible, of course, only because the conductors had at their disposal a vastly experienced ensemble, however small, appearing in productions modelled on those of the German theaters in which the principals had sung, often enough with each other. This would be especially true of the *Ring* productions, as close as possible to carbon copies of those of Bayreuth, where Seidl had worked as one of Wagner's assistants. It should be noted, too, that there were only four performances a week, on Monday, Wednesday and Friday evenings and a Saturday matinée, leaving Tuesdays and Thursdays free for rehearsal.

But if what the conductors did suggests the prodigious, we arrive, with the singers, at the fabulous, most notably in the accomplishments of Marianne Brandt, Amalie Materna and, above all, Lilli Lehmann, who joined the company in its second season and remained through its sixth and next to last.

The heroines of the first season were Materna and Brandt, who had shared the role of Kundry in the first performances of *Parsifal* at Bayreuth in 1882. Brandt, whose voice would seem to have defied categorization, sang nine roles: Leonore in *Fidelio*, Hedwig in *William Tell*, Ortrud in *Lohengrin*, Donna Elvira in *Don Giovanni*, Fidès in *Le Prophète*, Maddalena in *Rigoletto*, Fricka and Gerhilde in *Die Walküre* and Rachel in *La Juive*, averaging a performance every three days.

Materna, who had sung the three Brünnhildes in the first *Ring* at Bayreuth in 1876, joined the company as Elisabeth in *Tannhäuser* on 5 January, and went on to sing seventeen performances in forty-seven days as Rachel, Valentine in *Les Huguenots* and the *Die Walküre* Brünnhilde, averaging a performance every two and a half days. Both Materna and Brandt enjoyed a rapturous public and critical acclaim.

Not all the heroics were on the distaff side. The company's principal tenor, Anton Schott, excited less rapture, but what he demonstrated in terms of vocal and physical stamina excites our own incredulity. In ninety-seven days he sang forty-four performances, an average of a performance every two days, or close to it. His roles were Tannhäuser, Florestan, Lohengrin, John of Leyden, Masaniello (*La Muette di Portici*), Raoul (*Les Huguenots*) and Siegmund.

Materna did not return. In her place came Lehmann from Berlin, who made her debut as Carmen (!) on 25 November 1885, one day after her thirty-seventh birthday. That she next appeared five days later as the Brünnhilde of *Die Walküre* (her first; she had sung Fricka in Berlin!), and followed this on 2 December with Sulamith in the first American production of *The Queen of Sheba*, offered a hint of what might be expected of this extraordinary woman.

In the course of her five seasons with the company she was to sing twenty-one roles in nineteen operas, in *Die Walküre* singing both Brünnhilde and Sieglinde and in *The Queen of Sheba* both Sulamith and the Queen. This was, to be sure, only a fraction of a repertoire that embraced well over 100 operas, 114 according to an appendix to her autobiography, *Mein Weg*.

The high point of her residence was reached, of course, with the first American production of the *Ring* in the season of 1888/89, when she sang all three Brünnhildes, that of *Götterdämmerung* for the first time. Thus, she sang in *Die Walküre* on 5 March, *Siegfried* on 8 March and *Götterdämmerung* on 11 March, throwing in a Rachel on 9 March for good measure. As the season neared its end, she sang the Brünnhildes of *Götterdämmerung* on 16 March, *Siegfried* on 20 March and *Götterdämmerung* on 21 March (matinée) and again on 22 March.

The following season, 1889/90, was Lehmann's last with this ensemble, and she gave New York something new to remember her by in a single "benefit" performance of *Norma* on 27 February (she had previously sung Adalgisa in Berlin). As Henry Krehbiel put it in the *Tribune*: "No one can have followed the doings at the Metropolitan Opera House without having reached the conclusion long ago that a tremendously large proportion of the proud achievements of that institution have been directly due to the genius and devotion of that marvellously gifted woman."

There are others whose names deserved to be inscribed in a Hall of Fame of those seven seasons alongside those of Materna, Brandt and Lehmann. When *Tristan und Isolde* had its American premiere on 1 December 1886, Lehmann's Tristan was Albert Niemann, who had been the Tannhäuser of Wagner's Parisian fiasco of 1861 and the first Bayreuth Siegmund. When he made his Metropolitan debut in the latter role on 10 November 1886, he was 56, and celebrated his fifty-seventh birthday on 15 January 1887. His career had already covered thirty-eight years, and yet in this and the next season he also sang Florestan, Tannhäuser, John of Leyden, Lohengrin, Éleazar, Fernand Cortez and the *Götterdämmerung* Siegfried.

Then there was Emil Fischer, most noted as America's first and, until Friedrich Schorr's arrival forty years later, its greatest Hans Sachs. In his six seasons with the company he appeared in twenty-eight roles, including the three Wotans, Hagen and King Mark. He, too, was no youngster, having been born in 1838. He took to New York and settled there as a teacher.

But with the season of 1890/91 came the Götterdämmerung, and it was not Wagner's. Lehmann had warned Seidl and his manager, Edmond C. Stanton, that the repertoire was overloaded with Wagner. As Eduard Hanslick had put it when Hans von Bülow and his Meiningen Orchestra repeated Beethoven's Ninth Symphony, it was a case of baptizing the infidels with a fire hose.

Lehmann, Brandt, Materna and Niemann were gone. The Wagner canon was complete except for *Parsifal*, still restricted to Bayreuth. The premieres of that last season make sorry reading: *Asrael* by Baron Alberto Franchetti; Antonio Smareglia's *Il vassallo di Szigeth*, and, finally, Ernst II, Duke of Saxe-Coburg-Gotha's *Diana von Solange*. The last flicker was Minnie Hauk's Carmen toward the end of the season.

The next season was under the aegis of Abbey, John B. Schoeffel and Maurice Grau. It opened with Emma Eames and the De Reszkes singing *Roméo et Juliette* in French. Lilli Lehmann was back two evenings later singing Leonora in *Il trovatore* – in Italian. It was the end of an era and the beginning of a new. But what an era it had been! It is probably not abusing hyperbole to say that it was unique in the annals of opera.

13

The Vienna Decade

I F the German seasons at the Met in the 1880s represented a unique ensemble achievement for the nineteenth century, the accomplishments of the Vienna State Opera in the decade 1945–55 represent a similar one for the twentieth. Indeed, the Vienna experience was even more remarkable, given the extraordinary military, political and economic circumstances under which it evolved.

I cannot, of course, speak of what took place in New York in the 1880s at first hand, nor is there phonographic evidence to support or contradict the written evidence of those who experienced those productions in person. But for what took place in Vienna I can call on my own memory and on the oral and written memories of others. As far as purely musical/vocal accomplishments are concerned, there is an abundance of supporting, qualifying or contradictory evidence on disc and tape.

The battle for Vienna ended on 14 April 1945. From that date until 1 September, the city was occupied by the Soviet Army. Thereafter, and until the implementation of the State Treaty in 1955, Vienna was quadripartitely occupied by the Americans, British, French and Russians, each of the four being assigned an occupation zone of its own. As of 27 April, there was a Provisional Austrian Government under the chancellorship of Dr Karl Renner. This was succeeded on 25 November by a democratically elected coalition government headed by the conservative Leopold Figl as chancellor, the socialist Adolf Schaerf as vice-chancellor and Dr Renner, a socialist, as president.

Commander-in-Chief of the United States Forces in Austria (USFA) and American High Commissioner was General Mark W. Clark. He was succeeded in 1947 by General Geoffrey Keyes. Liaison between the High Commissioner and the Austrian government was conducted for General Clark by Lt Col Edwin M.J. Kretzmann, with me, a major, as his deputy. Under General Keyes, it was carried on by me until my departure for Germany in 1950. Throughout that period, avocationally and in my off-duty hours, I covered the musical scene in Vienna and the Salzburg Festivals for the *New York Times*.

As the State Opera, especially in the early years, required extensive support from the occupying powers in the form of fuel, electricity, material of various kinds and travel documentation, not to mention the solution of problems arising from often conflicting de-Nazification policies and procedures – decisions of the Allied Council had to be unanimous! – I was inevitably a witness to, and sometimes a participant in, much of what went on behind the scenes. My concern here, however, is with what took place before our eyes and ears in the theater.

I would not venture an account of that operatic decade depending on memory alone, vividly remembered as much of it is. Fortunately, I can now draw on a book, *Die Wiener Staatsoper im Exil*, compiled by Herbert Hackenberg and Walter Herrmann, published by the Oesterreicher Bundesverlag, G.m.b.H., in 1985, containing the dates, casting and number of performances of every production mounted in that decade, including the conductors, producers and designers, and even the number of appearances made by each singer in a major role and each conductor in that production.

The book's title requires some explanation. It does not refer to a State Opera exiled from Austria or even from Vienna, but merely transferred from proper residence in its home on the Ringstrasse, destroyed in an Allied bombing raid on Vienna on 12 March 1945, first to the Volksoper, a mile or so away on the Währingergürtel and subsequently to a quickly restored Theater an der Wien, only a few hundred yards away from the Ringstrasse, where Beethoven's *Fidelio* had first been seen and heard in 1805. It had recently served more humbly as a warehouse.

Thanks to this reservoir of statistical information, I can report that during the decade under review, playing nightly in two houses, the Volksoper and the Theater an der Wien, the State Opera mounted more than 120-odd new productions, sixty-odd in each house. I use approximate figures because some productions played in both houses, some were remounted or transferred from the Volksoper to the Theater an der Wien, others not, and finally because the totals given include occasional performances in the Redoutensaal of the Hofburg and the company's visits to various Western European cities. Figures I shall be giving for the number of performances by individual singers and conductors will similarly be approximations, close enough for the purposes of this account, but not to be accepted as exact.

The number of new productions in a decade would challenge credulity for any company in the world at any time. The standard of the performances in repertoire – not just star-studded premieres – could not, with few exceptions and only occasionally, be matched anywhere today, and had quite possibly not been matched previously on such a scale over so long a period. What makes the achievement even more astonishing is that it began from scratch.

The last official performance at the old Staatsoper had been a *Götterdämmerung* under Hans Knappertsbusch on 30 June 1944. All theaters in Germany and Austria were closed for the duration as of August 1944. The company was disbanded, the personnel scattering as suited their threatened convenience. The ravages of war had destroyed not only the Staatsoper on the Ringstrasse, but scenery, costumes, properties, wigs, etc.

And yet, by order of the Russians, on 1 May 1945, in a city without public transport or street lighting, and with a population subsisting on a rationed 800 calories a day, the State Opera was reborn with a performance of *Le nozze di Figaro* at the Volksoper. It was sung in German, as had been the custom in the past, and as would be true of all productions in this decade, with the unsuccessful and inconsistent exceptions of *Aida* and *La traviata*.

This inaugural production was conducted by Anton Paulik who, in June, would pass the baton to Joseph Krips, but would continue as the guiding spirit for light opera and operetta at the Volksoper, conducting twenty-six new productions a total of 971 times. It was staged by Oskar Fritz Schuh, who continued as director of productions throughout the decade. The hastily assembled cast offered a foretaste of what lay in store.

The Countess was Hilde Konetzni, destined to sing 339 performances of fourteen leading lyric-dramatic soprano roles. The Susanna was Irmgard Seefried, wife of the orchestra's concertmaster, Wolfgang Schneiderhahn. She went on to sing ninety-eight more Susannas among her 389 appearances in fifteen new productions. The Cherubino was the 23-year-old Sena Jurinac, making a debut with the company. She made the role pretty much her own, singing it another 117 times.

The Count was Alfred Poell, as he would be 118 times again as part of a contribution that included 623 appearances in twenty-four roles. The Figaro was Alois Pernerstorfer, a utility bass-baritone. He shortly gave way to Erich Kunz, who was to sing Figaro an astonishing total of 146 times. Similarly, Hermann Gallos as Basilio was succeeded by Peter Klein, who, as the company's principal "Spieltenor", sang the role 133 times (to go along with his

118 Servants in *Les Contes d'Hoffmann* and 109 Monostatoses in *Die Zauberflöte*).

Even more astonishing was the appearance of Elisabeth Höngen as Marcellina. She was to be the company's memorable Brangäne, Amneris, Fricka, Klytemnestra, Octavian, Azucena and Carmen. She sang Marcellina another forty-two times.

I dwell at such length on this *Le nozze di Figaro* because the casting, and the number of times certain singers were to appear in certain roles, reflect the emphasis on standards and ensemble that was to be the decade's most distinctive and admirable characteristic, achievable only through the selfless dedication of the artists involved – not to mention the fact that travel at the time was difficult and often impossible.

Vivid in my memory as an example is the production of *Die Zauberflöte* with a cast that I give here along with the number of times each singer appeared in the role in the course of the decade. The Pamina was Seefried (44), Tamino was Dermota (65), the Queen of the Night was Vilma Lipp (124), Sarastro was Ludwig Weber (37), Papageno was Kunz (81), Papagena was Emmy Loose (158), the Speaker was Schöffler (50), Monostatos was Klein (109), First Lady was Ljuba Welitsch (34), Second Lady Jurinac (21) and Third Lady Höngen (37). When a company can offer Welitsch, Jurinac and Höngen as the three Ladies, it is not only rich in personnel, but thrice blessed.

The ensemble goal had been defined at the very outset by Alfred Jerger, a veteran bass-baritone who had been with the company since 1921, and had sung something in the order of 150 roles, upon his appointment by the Russians as provisional director toward the end of April 1945 (Franz Salmhofer was to take over as director upon the move to the Theater an der Wien):

"We are dedicated to the task of giving back to Vienna its opera, if for the time being in a different and simplified form. One must not forget that the institution's material resources have been totally wiped out. The scenery is gone, the costumes, wigs, shoes, stage props, in short, everything that is required for luxuriant productions. We need new scenery, new costumes, but for that we lack basic materials. We must make do with the most modest means. Audiences, accordingly, as far as what is to be seen on the stage, must be content with mere hints, possibly with improvisation. But if in such matters we are compelled to compromise, there will be no compromising when it comes to artistic achievement. About that I am certain. The high standards reached through an artistic tradition will be preserved by the idealism of every individual artist."

During May of 1945 performances were given only every second day, and because there was neither public transportation nor street lighting, curtain time was three o'clock in the afternoon. Beginning on 1 June, performances were given daily. Casting continued to be governed by who was in Vienna and could get to the house, also by who could get to Vienna. The company was fortunate in its local nucleus.

The second new production was *La Bohème* on 15 May, produced by Jerger and conducted by Paulik, with Jurinac as Mimi and Seefried as Musetta. This premiere brought back to the company the stylish Slovenian tenor Anton Dermota as Rodolfo. He would contribute to the distinctions of the decade 743 appearances in thirty-three operas, including sixty-eight Don Ottavios, sixty-five Taminos, fifty-nine Hoffmanns, fifty-four Almavivas and forty-two Ferrandos.

Lortzing's *Der Waffenschmied* was added to the repertoire on 2 June. Three days later Johann Strauss's *Wiener Blut* was given in the Redoutensaal. Both were conducted by Paulik, the latter with Jurinac as the Countess in a cast reinforced by guests from the Raimundtheater and the Burgtheater. *Wiener Blut* was to have 211 performances, sixty-two in the Redoutensaal and 151 in the Volksoper. Jerger sang Count Ypsheim 125 times, Fritz Krenn the Kagler 159 and Kunz the Josef 118.

More important for the future was *Il barbiere di Siviglia* on 14 June, if only because it brought back to Vienna Joseph Krips (1902–74). Not only henceforth as the principal conductor of the State Opera, but also as conductor of the Vienna Philharmonic (a selection from the orchestra of the State Opera), he was the guiding musical spirit and executant of the decade.

A protégé of Felix Weingartner, Krips had begun his career as conductor in Aussig an der Elbe and Dortmund and as a very young general music director at Karlsruhe. He had been brought to Vienna by Clemens Krauss in 1933. At the time of the Anschluss in 1938, he was compelled to leave for racial reasons, and found employment briefly as Kapellmeister in Belgrade. Following the German invasion of Yugoslavia, he worked secretly as a coach, and many of those singers who would subsequently contribute so vitally to the distinctive post-war Mozart productions owed their stylistic security to him.

A week later, with *Madama Butterfly*, came the re-emergence of the Italianate (if not Italian) dramatic soprano in the person of the Serbian Daniza Ilitsch. She had enjoyed considerable success before and during the war in Berlin and Vienna. Just at the end, she had narrowly escaped the dire consequences of harbouring a British agent. Only the capture of Vienna by the Soviet Army had released her from prison and a summons to appear before a People's Court. The Pinkerton (Linkerton in German) was the Bulgarian tenor Wenko Wenkoff, destined to sing 422 performances in twenty-one productions as a principal standby tenor, mostly in the Italian repertoire, but including seventy appearances in *Eine Nacht in Venedig*. The Sharpless was Schöffler.

All the foregoing was essentially a run-up to the move to the Theater an der Wien, appropriately celebrated with a new production on 6 October of *Fidelio*, conducted by Krips, staged by Schuh and designed by Robert Kautsky. In the cast were Hilde Konetzni's sister Anny in the title role, Willy Franter as Florestan, Schöffler as Pizarro, Herbert Alsen as Rocco, Seefried as Marzellina, Dermota as Jacquino and Krenn as the Minister.

The Florestan was to have been Max Lorenz, who had been to German-speaking central Europe during the Nazi period what Lauritz Melchior had been to English-speaking audiences, only with a far wider non-Wagnerian repertoire, but he was held up at the demarcation line between the Russian and American Zones and arrived only in time to join the audience for Act II. He took over the role – memorably – at the next performance, and went on to sing it another thirty-nine times. In Anny Konetzni the company now had a true German dramatic soprano who would go on to sing twenty-seven more Leonores, fifteen Elektras, thirty-three Marschallins, twenty-four Isoldes and sixteen *Die Walküre* Brünnhildes.

Fidelio was to remain a pillar of the repertoire both at home and on tour, enjoying 153 performances. Among the conductors, in addition to Krips, were Rudolf Kempe, Rudolf Moralt, Hans Knappertsbusch, Karl Böhm, Clemens Krauss, Wilhelm Furtwängler, Otto Ackermann and Erich Leinsdorf. Other Leonores included Hilde Konetzni, Helena Braun, Christl Goltz, Maria Reining, Martha Mödl and the young Leonie Rysanek. Florestan was shared by Lorenz with Julius Patzak, Gunther Treptow, Torsten Ralf, Peter Anders, Set Svanholm, Helge Rosvaenge, Hans Hopf and Wolfgang Windgassen. It makes heady reading – and made heady hearing, too!

Three weeks after the *Fidelio* came a new production of *Les Contes d'Hoffmann*, again with Krips, Schuh and Kautsky in charge, and with Dermota in the title role, which he would share largely, but not exclusively, with Patzak. The four bass-baritone roles were taken by Schöffler. Many others followed him, most notably, after 1949, George London with twenty-nine performances. It was this role that established the young American not only as an artist of international stature, but also as a matinee idol of a kind unknown in Vienna since the prime of Jan Kiepura.

The four female roles were all sung at the premiere by Seefried. It was a mistake, and she confined herself thereafter to Antonia and Stella, sharing the roles with Jurinac. Olympia was sung most often by Lipp and Loose, Giulietta by Hilde Konetzni and Welitsch. The production was to have 182 performances.

Other new productions during what was left of 1945 included, at the Volksoper, *Tosca* with Ilitsch (later most frequently with Welitsch), Wilhelm Kienzl's *Der Evangelimann* (bringing the splendid Hungarian mezzo Rosette Anday back to the company), *Hänsel und Gretel* (with Anny Konetzni as the mother!), *Die Fledermaus*, *Don Pasquale* (with the same cast as in 1942–44) and *Cavalleria rusticana* and *Pagliacci* (the latter with Schwarzkopf as Nedda).

At the Theater an der Wien the year came to a memorable close with *Otello*, again with the Krips–Schuh–Kautsky trio in charge, and with Max Lorenz in the title role, Schöffler as Iago, Hilde Konetzni as Desdemona and Elena Nikolaidi as Emilia. The critic of *Die Weltpresse* called this production and performance "a landmark in the opera history of a re-born Austria", and this was not reckless hyperbole or chauvinism. Others wrote in the same vein.

Lorenz's Otello, in particular, was hailed as a masterpiece of vocal and theater art, and I echo that verdict. My Otellos have included Zenatello, Martinelli, Renato Gigli, Del Monaco, Vinay, Vickers and McCracken, and I have no hesitation in naming Lorenz as the most convincing and most moving of them all, even singing the role in German. He was to offer it at the Theater an der Wien another fifty-three times. Schöffler, too, I would rate as the finest of the Iagos I have experienced. Konetzni was to share Desdemona with Maria Reining, both superb.

It seems appropriate at the year's end to recall that the State Opera, in only eight months, beginning from scratch, without scenery, costumes or props, in a city without public transport or street lighting and a citizenry subsisting on 800, later 1200 calories a day, often without gas or electricity, with a nucleus of staff and artistic personnel limited initially to those who happened to be in Vienna at the war's end, had staged eighteen new productions in two houses and achieved a standard of performance probably unequalled at the time anywhere else.

The first six months of 1946 brought new productions of *Rigoletto* (Georg Oeggl sharing the title role with the young Giuseppe Taddei), *Tristan und Isolde* (with Lorenz and Anny Konetzni), *Salome* (with Welitsch making opera history in the title role and with Lorenz and Höngen matchless as Herod and Herodias) and *Pique Dame* (with Höngen, Hilde Konetzni, Lorenz and Schöffler). Subsequent casting of *Pique Dame* was no less strong with Patzak, Welitsch, Margarete Klose, Anday among others.

By now and henceforward, the company was constantly reinforced by established singers from Germany, drawn partly by the company's already impressive record, partly because Austria, as a liberated rather than vanquished nation, was a more congenial residence and scene of activity than Germany, with most of its opera houses in ruins, or, in some cases, as a refuge from the more severe de-Nazification measures imposed by the occupying powers in the now defunct Third Reich.

Among the arrivals, some of them already named in these pages, were many native Viennese: Hilde Güden, Gertrude Grob-Prandl, Georg Hann, Fritz Krenn, Julius Patzak, Julius Pölzer and Ludwig Weber. Others included Ljuba Welitsch, Maria Cebotari, Christl Goltz, Elisabeth Grümmer, Ludwig Hofmann, Helena Braun and her husband, Ferdinand Frantz, Max Lorenz, Hans Hotter, Gottlob Frick, Gunther Treptow and Helge Rosvaenge. They all stayed, and some of them were awarded Austrian citizenship with eyebrow-raising alacrity. Little by little the conducting burden was shared by Krips and Moralt with Clemens Krauss, Otto Ackermann, Karl Böhm and Hans Knappertsbusch.

An account of the last six months of 1946 again makes astonishing reading: new productions of *Der Rosenkavalier* on 13 September; *Tannhäuser* (at the Volksoper) on 20 September; *Don Giovanni* on 13 October; *Die Entführung aus dem Serail* on 20 October; *Die Walküre* on 2 December and *Aida* (in Italian) on 12 December. Most significant for the future reputation of the State Opera in that decade were the two Mozart premieres and *Der Rosenkavalier*, as Mozart and Strauss were to provide the *pièces de resistance* for the company's impending tours.

Don Giovanni was cast with Schöffler in the title role, Kunz as Leporello, Dermota as Don Ottavio, Welitsch as Donna Anna, Hilde Konetzni as Donna Elvira, Seefried as Zerlina, Poell as Masetto and Weber as the Commendatore. This production was to have 155 performances. Schöffler shared the title role with Poell and, after 1949, with George London.

Die Entführung had almost the same cast as the last performances in 1944: Elisabeth Schwarzkopf as Konstanze, Loose as Blondchen, Dermota as

Belmonte and Klein as Pedrillo. Only Weber as Osmin was new to the cast. There was subsequently no shortage of Osmins: Alsen, Endre Koreh, Hofmann, Frick and Kurt Böhme. Konstanze was passed to Lipp, and Dermota shared Belmonte with Patzak, Ludwig and, for one performance, Rosvaenge.

Der Rosenkavalier, conducted by Moralt, staged by Jerger and designed by Kautsky after Alfred Roller, was again ideally cast, and in similar depth. Anny Konetzni (premiere) shared the Marschallin with her sister and Vienna-born Maria Reining (the latter, in my opinion, and not mine alone, the most sympathetic and moving of all in that role). Höngen (premiere) shared Oktavian with Jurinac (the latter my preference over any other). Loose shared Sophie with Güden and Lisa della Casa (who also sang a single Oktavian). The Ochs was Weber, the role then to be shared with Fritz Krenn. The Faninal was Karl Kamann, who was to sing him sixty-three times. Dermota was the Italian singer, as he would be on thirty-eight other occasions. He was not quite the best of many. Rosvaenge was.

Tannhäuser had Lorenz in the title role, with Hilde Konetzni as Elisabeth and her sister as Venus. *Die Walküre* had Lorenz, again, as Siegmund, Hilde Konetzni as Sieglinde, her sister as Brünnhilde (what would the State Opera have done without those Konetzni sisters?), Hotter as Wotan and Höngen as Fricka. Subsequent Siegmunds included Treptow, Ludwig Suthaus, Ralf and Wolfgang Windgassen.

By the close of 1946, the work of building a basic repertoire and assembling a largely resident company was essentially complete, and the company could now embark on the tours that would do more than anyone might initially have imagined possible to establish the new Austria's identity favourably in the community of European nations. These tours took the Vienna State Opera to Nice and London in 1947, to Antwerp in 1948, to Milan, Florence, Paris, Brussels, Amsterdam and the Hague in 1949, to Brussels in 1950, to Paris in 1951, to Paris and Brussels in 1952, to Wiesbaden, Brussels and Paris in 1953 and to Wiesbaden, Brussels and London in 1954.

The repertoire on tour was predominantly but not exclusively Mozart. *Salome* was added for London – and Welitsch – and *Fidelio* in 1947; *Der Rosenkavalier* for Brussels and Amsterdam in 1949; *Tristan und Isolde* and *Fidelio* for Paris in 1951; *Wozzeck* for Paris in 1952 (with Theo Hermann and Goltz); *Der Rosenkavalier* for Wiesbaden and Brussels, and *Elektra* and *Die Liebe der Danae* for Paris in 1953 and *L'elisir d'amore* for Brussels in 1954.

These tours inevitably brought international recognition and acclaim to the company's principal singers; and as travel restrictions were eased toward the end of the 1940s some of them began to accept engagements elsewhere, in Germany, Italy, France, England, Switzerland and America. But so rich was the company in highly qualified artists for just about every leading role that absences were easily accommodated, and even opened the way for new and budding talent.

Of the many new productions in the years after 1946 I shall note only those that remain most vividly fixed in my memory. In 1947 we had *Ariadne auf Naxos* (with Reining and Cebotari sharing the title role and Seefried and Jurinac the Composer); *Boris Godunov* (with Schöffler and Weber and, after 1950, London); *Prince Igor* (with Schöffler) and *La traviata* (with Schwarzkopf and Cebotari).

In 1948 we had *Turandot* (with Cebotari and Grob-Prandl, and with Rosvaenge as an unrivalled Calaf) and *Die Zauberflöte* (with the cast I have given elsewhere). Finally, during my residence, in 1949, came *Die Meistersinger* (with Schöffler an unforgettable Sachs and Kunz a matchless Beckmesser).

The decade and the era came to an end with the return to the rebuilt Staatsoper on the Ringstrasse in 1955. The company would continue to flourish, but without duplicating the unique atmosphere that gave opera, and especially Mozart, an intimacy and charm associated exclusively with the acoustical and physical environment of the Theater an der Wien. As an opera-lover, I was immensely fortunate to find myself, thanks to the vicissitudes and vagaries of war, in the right place at the right time. It is unlikely that the accomplishments of that decade in Vienna will ever be equalled.

14

Record – or Perish: Giuseppina Cobelli – a Personal Memoir

IN early May of 1945, as an intelligence officer on the staff of the American Fifth Army at our final headquarters in Gardone on the western shore of the Lago di Garda, I was billeted in a small hotel, or *pensione*, just south of the town and right on the lakeshore. The hotel was called the *Spiaggia d'Oro*, or Beach of Gold. A week or so after we had settled in, I was told by one of the servant girls that our proprietress had been a famous opera singer whose career had been cut short by deafness. I asked her name, fairly confident that if this lady had truly been so famous, her name would be familiar to me. It was given: Giuseppina Cobelli. I had never heard of her.

I had been music critic of the Philadelphia *Evening Bulletin* from 1930 to 1942 at a time when the Met came to Philadelphia twenty-two Tuesday evenings every season. I was familiar with the names and the art of such Italian prima donnas as Claudia Muzio, Maria Caniglia, Gina Cigna, Licia Albanese and Hilde Reggiani, and had heard on record or read about others who never sang at the Met.

I was, understandably, I think, skeptical. Our proprietress, certainly, did not look the part – a sturdy, plumpish blonde, indifferently dressed and coiffured, hardly distinguishable from other middle-aged landladies as she rode her bicycle into town, a grocery basket on the handlebars, to make the purchases for the small villa she owned and occupied immediately adjacent to the hotel. She kept to herself. Indeed, we saw her only on the bicycle, or as she walked from the hotel to her villa and back, or through the window of her office, seated at her desk and working at her accounts. I watched her through that window, one morning, her back to the door, when one of the servant girls entered to ask a question. There was no response. I knew that our proprietress was not only hard of hearing. She was deaf.

Toward the end of May, I was in Milan, and privileged to be shown through the ruins of La Scala. One of my first questions to our guides and other theater personnel was, naturally: "What can you tell me about a singer named Giuseppina Cobelli?" The response was explosive. "Cobelli? Our greatest

Santuzza, our greatest Isolde, our greatest Gioconda, our greatest Sieglinde, our greatest Fedora, our greatest Adriana Lecouvreur", and so on through the dramatic soprano repertoire. (Now, forty-five years later, one can learn from a variety of lexicons that Giuseppina Cobelli was born on 1 August 1898 at Maderno on the Lago di Garda and made her debut as Gioconda at Piacenza in 1924. She sang for a season with an Italian company in Holland, and joined La Scala as Sieglinde in 1925, remaining with the company until 1942, especially noted for her Wagnerian and *verismo* roles.)

I knew immediately that I must make our proprietress's acquaintance, and learn more about a singer who could excite such ardent superlatives, but whose name and reputation had remained unknown on my side of the Atlantic, or anywhere else outside Italy. Our paths crossed a day or so later, and I introduced myself not only as an American officer temporarily billeted in her hotel, but also as an American music critic and opera-lover from Philadelphia. She responded politely but coldly. As a hotel proprietress she had had enough of war and of requisitioning, first by Germans and now by Americans, with no certainty as to when or how, or by how much, she would be recompensed. Her policy, obviously, was to do what was required by the requisitioners, keep her mouth shut, mind her own business, stay out of trouble, and hope for better times ahead.

But I persisted, and in a matter of days the ice melted, or at least began to melt, as she satisfied herself that I was, or had been, what I said I was, that I knew quite a lot about opera and opera singers, had heard much and was a personal friend of singers well known to her. It helped, too, that I could bring her news of such former colleagues as Giuseppe de Luca, Ferrucio Tagliavini, Pia Tassinari, Gino Bechi and Titta Ruffo whom I had met during our wartime progress up the Italian peninsula from Salerno to Gardone.

Conversation was not easy. She spoke neither English nor German, and, although she had a hearing aid, she didn't like it, and didn't use it. She once showed it to me, saying, "Questa è la mia croce!" But my Italian was reasonably fluent in those days, and as a former budding baritone I have a resonant voice. As a former newscaster I know how to pace my speech and enunciate distinctly. Face-to-face, things went well enough. If her back was turned, she heard nothing.

That the ice had really been broken was signaled to me one day in June when she invited me to her villa for tea. The villa was small. Downstairs there were just a living room and a dining room, modestly, plainly furnished, with a baby grand piano taking up much of the limited space. I had rather expected as much. What I had not expected was the almost total absence of relics, souvenirs or other reminders of an illustrious career.

In the living room of a once-famous prima donna one usually finds the piano cluttered with photos of herself in her great roles and autographed photos of colleagues, the walls decorated with playbills of premieres and other notable occasions. Here there was nothing but a single full-length oil painting of Giuseppina as Isolde, her fully rounded arms outstretched, presumably singing the "Liebestod" – in Italian, of course.

It was the same with her conversation. We saw much of one another in the following weeks, but only rarely did she refer to the events and accomplishments of the past. It often seemed to me that the deafness that had ended her career had also shut out her memories of the sounds she had once made and heard – or any desire to remember them. That impression is strengthened by the fact that she had apparently forgotten – or chosen to forget – ever having made a recording.

It was only some years later that I learned from my friend Max de Schauensee, who had succeeded me as music critic of the Philadelphia *Evening Bulletin*, that she had, in fact, made two – and only two: 'Voi lo sapete" from *Cavalleria rusticana* and the "Suicidio" from *La Gioconda*, recorded on separate acoustic HMV sides in 1924/5. Max played these now very rare 78s for me, and glorious recordings they are! Her failure to record thereafter, or to appear in England or North America, doubtless explains why her name and reputation, even when her career was at its height, were so little known abroad.

Giuseppina Cobelli was well remembered, however, by her former colleagues, as documented in Lanfranco Rasponi's *The Last Prima Donnas* (1982). Gianna Pederzini, recalling her first La Scala appearance as the Princesse de Bouillon in *Adriana Lecouvreur* in 1932, told Rasponi: "Cobelli was the protagonist, and her magic will never be equalled, despite a peculiar voice and a short top." Of Cobelli's Eboli (she had been chosen for the part by Toscanini for the La Scala revival of *Don Carlo* in 1926, when she was 28), Pederzini said: "The *tessitura* is very tricky, and in fact no one was more superb than Cobelli, who was a dramatic soprano."

Ebe Stignani substituted for an ailing Cobelli as Eboli in 1926 and remembered: "I was in a panic. First of all, Cobelli was a beautiful woman – and there never was a kinder one, either – a tremendous favourite, and had made the role her own despite the fact that she was a soprano. . . . Here I was taking someone else's place, and it is difficult to imagine today what her position was then."

Maria Caniglia said of her: "She was a most exceptional person, both as an artist and as a woman, and took me under her protection. Whenever she could, she came to my performances, made notes, and the next day telephoned me to pass on her impressions, both positive and negative. They were invaluable to me, for no one had a greater sense of the theatre. . . . Her unforgettable Isolde was the barrier that precluded me from ever accepting this divine role."

According to Augusta Oltrabella, a contemporary at La Scala, "Cobelli, the most superb of all the artists I heard, had a sumptuous voice, the warmest timbre I can recall, with a splendid B flat. But there it stopped. The C never came despite every effort on her part. She was exceedingly intelligent, and she learned to live with it."

Dame Eva Turner, who sang with Cobelli during two seasons at the Teatro Colón in Buenos Aires, remembers her as "a superb Isolde and at the same time thrilling as Tosca and Eboli." And Mafalda Favero: "Giuseppina Cobelli's Isolde and Katiusha in [Alfano's] *Risurrezione* absolutely always tore me apart, and I was grateful for the pain she had made me suffer, a sort of cleansing and purification." Finally, Sara Scuderi, another La Scala contemporary: "Giuseppina Cobelli's Tosca paralyzed me with admiration."

To return to Gardone in the summer of 1945, it would seem that with deafness Giuseppina Cobelli had entered upon a new life in the present as proprietress of a *pensione*. It was upon this life that our conversation mostly centered, upon problems of finances, management, personnel, relationships with American and Italian officialdom, and so on. Once in a while the past would reappear briefly, just enough to enable me now to report that the roles closest to her heart were Silvana in Respighi's *La fiamma* (which she created in Rome in 1934), Fedora and Adriana Lecouvreur. Such moments of retrospection were rare.

During an evening we might listen to the radio or to records, although rarely to opera. I remember only one broadcast from Milan of the Gigli/Bruna Rasa recording of *Cavalleria rusticana* – with the volume high, of course – to which she listened with pleasure and admiration. Mostly we indulged in simpler fare, notably in the records of her favourite singer, Richard Tauber, also a favourite of mine. One Tauber recording in particular remains etched in my memory of those evenings: "Aus Apfelblüten einen Kranz" from *Das Land des Lächelns*.

Of her personal life Cobelli spoke little. I do remember, however, her telling me why she had never married: "I was totally dedicated to my work in the theater, and I could not ask any man whom I loved and admired to accept as little of my time and myself as I would have been prepared to give him." As to why she made no more recordings I can offer nothing at first hand, if only because she never made any reference to the two sides she did make in 1924/25. I can only surmise that, as the perfectionist she would seem to have been, she had not been entirely happy with what she heard.

She seemed to enjoy good health. I remember her once exclaiming, "Sono la donna più sana in tutt'Italia!" She wasn't. Shortly before the time came in early August for me to move on with General Mark Clark to Austria, she told me that she would have to go to the hospital for a minor gall-bladder operation. It was cancer, of which she died at nearby Barbarano di Salò on 2 September 1948.

15

The State of the (Vocal) Art

I SHOULD preface what follows by stressing that my listening experience during the past twenty-odd years has been confined almost wholly to what has come my way in London. But given the Royal Opera, the English National Opera and Glyndebourne, and the fact that today's outstanding singers constitute a kind of international touring company, with London an almost obligatory stop, I have probably heard most of those now enjoying international reputations. I do not speak of those I have heard on record. Cesare Siepi once told a friend of mine: "Don't believe anything you hear on records." I don't.

Among those singers who have emerged or achieved their highest standards since the end of World War II, pride of place goes, unquestionably in my view, to the tenors, although not, certainly, to Wagnerian tenors. A couple of generations that have produced or experienced the prime of Franco Corelli, Carlo Bergonzi, Nicolai Gedda, Giuseppe di Stefano, Alfredo Kraus, Jon Vickers, Placido Domingo, José Carreras, Luciano Pavarotti, Giacomo Aragall and James McCracken need offer no apologies to the vocal past. I have admired them all, and enjoyed them all.

If I were to single out one as standing somewhat above a distinguished company, it would be Domingo, whom I have been fortunate enough to hear often at the Royal Opera and on television, if in a relatively small sampling of his extraordinary repertoire. Listening to him, I almost invariably find myself asking: "Did Gigli, Martinelli, Pertile, Lauri-Volpi and Bjoerling sing any better?"

I heard them all except Pertile, whose singing I know only from his records, and I heard Gigli, Martinelli and Lauri-Volpi often, and in a variety of roles, and I think the answer might be a qualified "no". In some matters of style, taste, musicianship and immaculate vocalism they may not – as I remember them, and as I hear them today on record – have sung quite so well. But the voices were more individual, more distinctive and, in Gigli's case, more beautiful. Domingo's voice, goodness knows, falls mellifluously and persuasively upon the ear, but it hasn't quite the burnished silver quality of Gigli's, the incisive metal of Martinelli's, the ardour and fervour of Pertile's and the sensual insinuation of Lauri-Volpi's in his younger years, nor the sheer brilliance and intensity of Bjoerling's.

But I have treasured memories of all these more recent tenors: of Pavarotti's evident and contagious pleasure in the sound of his own effulgent voice, in the pleasure he knows it gives to others, and in his irrepressible and uninhibited, if self-indulgent, showmanship; of Bergonzi's innate and intuitive, if unabashedly Italianate, sense of style: of Kraus's elegance in movement, posture, attitude and enunciation; of Gedda's harmonization of warmth and refinement; of Carreras's native and richly voiced lyricism; of McCracken's deeply felt and vividly projected Otello (I wish that I might have been in New York for his Tannhäuser at the Met, of which I have heard only superlative accounts); of Vickers' Aeneas, Otello, Peter Grimes and Florestan, and so on.

If something is missing from this catalogue of tenor prosperity, it is the truly dramatic tenor. The last dominant figure in that category would be, I suppose, Mario del Monaco. All those named above, with the possible exception of Vickers, fall rather into the category of *spinto*, lyric tenors, as I have noted earlier, capable of undertaking successfully the dramatic roles, as Gigli, Pertile and Lauri-Volpi did. Of the true *Heldentenor* for the Wagnerian repertoire there has been none to efface or even challenge one's memories of Melchior, or of Max Lorenz in his prime. The same is true of Wagnerian sopranos. There has been only Nilsson and, more recently, Hildegarde Behrens to compete with our memories of Flagstad and Frida Leider.

Among baritones, with Tito Gobbi now gone, there have been only Sherrill Milnes, Renato Bruson and Piero Cappucilli to stand out among many excellent, if hardly legendary, singers. The standard among baritones is high (as is their vocal range), but they have not been of the kind, either as singers, actors, or personalities, whose names become household words.

The same would seem to be true of sopranos of all categories, many of them excellent – Kiri Te Kanawa the most vocally distinctive, Edita Gruberova the most vocally accomplished – in an opera world that remembers Callas and Beverly Sills and can still hear Joan Sutherland, Leontyne Price and Victoria de Los Angeles, if no longer in their vocal prime.

Some of us, of course, remember Maria Jeritza, Lucrezia Bori, Zinka Milanov, Rosa Ponselle, Rosa Raisa, Elisabeth Rethberg, Elisabeth Schumann, Bidu Sayão, Licia Albanese, Florence Easton and Eva Turner (the list could easily be extended), while in Italy and South America older operagoers have similarly vivid and as yet uneclipsed memories of Maria Caniglia, Gina Cigna, Giuseppina Cobelli, Mafalda Favero and Magda Olivero. This view might be disputed in North America on behalf of Renata Scotto, whose successes there I have not experienced.

Of true contraltos one can hardly speak, now that Kathleen Ferrier is only a memory. They seem to be an extinct species, although, curiously, and as I have noted elsewhere, almost all the finest female popular singers – Ella Fitzgerald, Sarah Vaughan, Peggy Lee and Cleo Laine, for example – are or have been contraltos right down to the low D. In their place we have mezzo-sopranos, themselves forever tempted, as Pasta, Malibran and Viardot – and, in my opinion, Callas and Jessye Norman – were, to shed the *mezzo* from their designation, and move up the scale vocally and financially.

Such has been the case with Grace Bumbry, Shirley Verrett and, from time to time, Janet Baker, the latter rejoicing in a command of coloratura (and the art of making it make musical sense) shared most conspicuously with Marilyn Horne, Teresa Berganza and, at the English National Opera, Della Jones. Frederica von Stade has so far resisted, or possibly not yet experienced, the upward urge, but she, too, is no more a true contralto than her sisters. It remains to be seen how far Maria Ewing will be tempted to follow her sisters up the vocal ladder. In the Italian repertoire my memories of Bruna Castagna, Ebe Stignani and Giulietta Simionato remain unchallenged, as do my memories of Karin Branzell, Kerstin Thorborg, Elisabeth Höngen, Rosette Anday and Margarete Klose in the German.

True basses, too, would seem to be an endangered species. We who remember in the flesh or on record Pol Plançon, Marcel Journet, Feodor Chaliapin, Adamo Didur, José Mardones, Léon Rothier, Ezio Pinza, Tancredi Pasero, Alexander Kipnis, Michael Bohnen and Ludwig Weber wonder whatever became of it. There are, today, fine basses aplenty, but they tend to be bass-baritones. They all have a high G, but sound as though nearing bottom at the low G. Among them, George London being no longer with us and Jerome Hines and Cesare Siepi nearing the end of splendid careers, Nicolai Ghiaurov, Martti Talvela, Hans Sotin, Kurt Moll and Robert Lloyd stand alone.

These past years have brought about a welcome widening of the opera repertoire by revivals of operas long lost to sight and hearing in the mists of 19th-century history. This is a singer's realm, and its successful recovery is primarily the singer's responsibility. Others may help. But the essential substance of this music is a melodic line. It is not enough that this line be sung merely correctly, in time and in tune. It must be shaped, varied, and embellished, and it must be sung persuasively, excitingly and convincingly. This will require more creative imagination and invention, more initiative and individuality, and greater self-respect and self-reliance than has been required – or permitted – of singers for most of this century. Callas, Sutherland, Horne and Caballé, among others, have shown the way.

Singers for whom this archaeology is attractive must become, to some extent, at least, musicologists. They must use libraries, consult old scores and pictures, learn to read in more than two clefs, study embellishment and the art of constructing effective and tasteful cadenzas, just as the instrumentalists do who are exploring the treasures of renaissance and baroque. And the singers have one great advantage. Old vocal recordings made by older artists going back to the turn of the century offer clues largely denied to the instrumentalist.

It is a paradox of the musical world as we near the end of the century that, while musicologists and some performers seek desperately to discover and revive the performance practices of the renaissance and baroque eras, no similar enthusiasm has yet been manifested for a similar investigation of the performance practices of the bel canto and romantic eras.

What makes this situation not only paradoxical, but almost farcical, is that whereas the musicologists and their performer colleagues seeking authenticity in the presentation of what is conveniently termed early music are doomed to uncertainty because they are deprived of any recorded aural evidence for their conclusions, our legacy of recorded evidence of performance practice in the 19th century, handed down by singers and instrumentalists who were, in many cases, the composers' contemporaries and more or less intimate colleagues and friends, is rich.

What that legacy offers us, more vividly and more accurately than musical notation or the prose of contemporary commentators and critics, is information about how the great arias and scenas of the baroque, bel canto and romantic eras were sung by singers far closer than we to the times and to the composers who produced them.

The sound we hear on those old records – thousands of them now easily available on LP and even CD transfers – is not, of course, the sound that the singers' listeners heard in opera house or concert hall, and the orchestral contributions are dreadful. But what we hear those singers do, they did. No splicing, filtering or enhancing in those days.

What comes through most compellingly on the records of the greatest of those singers – quite aside from technical accomplishment – is their individuality and authority, reflected not so much in notational liberties as in the moulding of line, the shaping of *portamenti*, the introduction of appoggiaturas and embellishments and the time taken for the vocal enrichment of phrase endings and cadences.

I remember playing one of Fernando de Lucia's famous recordings of "Ecco ridente" from *Il barbiere di Siviglia* for an eminent conductor of Central European origin, and his response: "Well, it's wonderful, but of course I wouldn't stand for it." In De Lucia's time it would have been the tenor who determined what would and would not be stood for. I remember, too, another conductor of similar background recalling how, at rehearsal, he kept yelling at Giacomo Lauri-Volpi: "Come scritto, come scritto!" Opera lovers of fifty or sixty years ago didn't pay to hear Lauri-Volpi singing "as written"!

What it all comes down to in the end is a question of style. The printed score or autograph tells us only what a composer wrote down, nothing about what, according to the conventions of his time, he left to the discretion of his performers, or expected or accepted from them, and consequently nothing about how his music sounded, or was expected to sound in his own time.

Literalness is easy, and today we have too much of it, often bordering on pedantry. Authenticity, on the other hand, is inseparable from style, as reflected in the art of those who projected the written score in the composer's own time, or close to it. This essential avenue of research is closed to students of the renaissance and baroque eras. It is open, thanks to those old 78s of the older singers, to students and performers of the bel canto and romantic eras.

The time has come then, I would suggest, for conductors – and singers, too – to add their ears to their eyes in the study of these old scores, using the old recordings as a guide. What is needed is a rediscovery and cultivation of the collaborative relationship of composer, singer and conductor which so distinguished the art of the great singers of the past and contributed so importantly to the vitality and longevity of the music they sang.

As far as enrichment from contemporary composition is concerned, there has been for the singer, also predictably, nothing worth discussion. There won't be until composers stop putting clusters of notes in singers' mouths that emerge less musically than the nuances and cadences of speech, and see their way clear, at long last, to give opera back to the singers, providing them with something to sing to their own and their listeners' hearts' content.

Index

INDEX